I0165759

Target

By D.A. McIntosh

Copyright© 2016 by David A. McIntosh
(D.A.McIntosh)

All rights reserved. No part of this book may be reproduced or
transmitted in any form or by any means, electronic or mechanical,
including photocopying, recording, or by any information storage
and retrieval system, without permission in writing from the
copyright owner.
Available through Amazon, Kindle and your local book store

This is a work of fiction. Names, characters, places and incidents
either are the product of the author's imagination or are fictitious,
and any resemblance to any actual persons, living or dead, events,
or locales is entirely coincidental.

Cover and Internal design© D.A.McIntosh
Cover photo by J.M. Owens (my grandfather, taken near the end of
World War I of the town of Ypres, Belgium)

ISBN 978-0-9856276-8-3

Dedication

As with all my books, I dedicate this one to the men and women who put their lives on the line every day, fighting for our freedom, protecting us and our property. They don't care where you come from, your religion, or color of your skin; if you need their help, they will be there to help you.

I thank the military, law enforcement and fire departments around the world for your dedication to service and sacrifices.

This book and the series can be purchased through Amazon and on your Kindle, and soon Audio books will be available on Amazon, Audible.com and iTunes

- *Chain of Deceit,* Book 1
- *Retribution,* Book 2
- *T - Minus 36,* Book 3
- *Final Report,* Book 4
- *Wounded Eagle,* Book 5
- *Schutzstaffel Rising,* Book 6
- *The Island* (Chain of Deceit)
- *Target*
- *Vengeance (coming soon)*

Table of Contents

Characters

Davin Pierce –Assistant Director CIA
Connie Pierce – FBI agent
Brian Forest – Militia Commander
Tony Sanford – President of the United States
Josh Randal – Director CIA
Stephanie Randal – wife of Director Randal, CIA Analysis
Rocky Soto – R&D scientist
Horatio Soto – Son of Rocky Soto
George Monahan, nickname 'Moose' - Mercenary
Sonja – Female Mercenary
Max the Mouse – Male Mercenary
Henry L. Rothchild – Investor
Richard Clark – Mercenary leader
Meredith Brown – Josh Randal's secretary and agent
Greg Conway – Lead Scientist working for Soto
Ulysses Robert "Bob" Green – Department Homeland Security (DHS)
Special Weapons and Tactics (SWAT) commander
Beth "Hawkeye" – DHS Sniper
Michelle "Snickers" – DHS Sniper
Chilly – German Shepherd Dog member of DHS
LT Bell – 2nd in command of DHS team
Mono Vale – Brian Forest's partner
Colonel Nelson Littleton – Battalion Commander US Marines
Tara Wong – aka Joanne Morgan, CIA Field Agent
Josh Pierce – son of Davin and Connie Pierce
Amber Pierce – twin sister to Josh
Bill Currumbin – Australian Navy Medic
Kyle Lasko – CIA Senior Field Agent
Captain Walter Phillips – Company Commander US Marines
Major Rhonda Olson – Pilot USAF transport aircraft
Sergeant Blake – crew chief on transport aircraft
Captain Stanis – USAF Pilot

Detective Captain Jon Wynn – Hong Kong Intelligence Agency
Sue Lynn – North Korean Prime Minister Bodyguard
Victoria – North Korean Prime Minister Bodyguard
Lieutenant Valerie 'Val' Lake – Hawaii Police Five O
Walter Kline – Director NSA
General Whitmore – General of the Army
General Brady – General of the Air Force

Preface

In late April of the year 2031, developments in technology had changed how people looked at the world, interacted, and spent their resources. Social media had grown over the years. Things like small implants in each human to replace cell phones, 4D virtual glasses, 3D printers producing everything from thumb tacks to human body parts and contact lenses to watch television and much more had made a major impact on the world.

Technology had reached an age that Hollywood once used to make into scary movies. With the genius minds of many engineers and with the use of superfast bio-technology, developers only needed to think of a project, and with the use of computer technology, they could produce it. Computers were able to do anything a human could do, only faster and with more precision. With the advancements in technology, crime and terrorism had not decreased; or for that matter, neither had it increased over the years. The advances had brought about better surveillance equipment to the point that many of the population felt that it was an invasion of privacy. The government, on the other hand, kept saying that without the surveillance of the world, crime and terrorism would increase and take over.

Back in 2016 in major cities such as New York, London, Los Angeles and many others, you could not walk down a street without being photographed hundreds if not thousands, of times. Technology had made it almost impossible to hide in any city on the planet but you could if you knew how to beat the system. Cellular phones, the invention of Hollywood with the communicator used by the actors of Star Trek had eventually progressed to a comm badge on their uniform, were utilized worldwide.

Today, 2031, an all-new cellular phone had emerged from technology begun about two decades earlier with a watch-like item that a person would wear on his or her wrist. The watch not only served as a timepiece, but also as an exercise monitor, calendar, and cell phone. To make a call, or answer one, all you had to do was tap the face and then hold your finger up to your ear with your thumb near your mouth. The signal would transmit through your body and you could talk and hear the conversation. The need for the wristband soon became obsolete for the phone. By placing an implant behind your ear, the person only had to tap their ear or click his/her jaw to answer, speak and listen without the use of any handheld or wrist device. Some companies still made the wrist device to monitor an individual's health, but cell phones had now evolved into implants. The implants also had a mini GPS on board which could pin point you to within three feet of your location. In case of an emergency, all you had to do was say a predetermined word, or tap your ear and say 'nine, one, one' to be connected to emergency services. The down side to this type of communication was that the government had the ability to track you no matter where, on earth, you were. There were still some places deep underground, in the depths of the ocean, or outside the earth's hemisphere that might enable you to be undetected, but even those areas were becoming fewer. Many people elected not to have the device implanted, stating it was an invasion of their privacy and they were correct. It was a choice, and the government had not made it mandatory, yet.

Other advances in technology were in the medical field. Cancer had been completely eliminated as a cause of death or debilitating disease; and many other killing diseases were now treatable. With the use of 3D technology, it was possible to create living human organs when a healthy replacement organ could not be located. This technology saved millions of people over the years; and as perfected, would save millions more. Life expectancy for the human race was upward to about one hundred and twenty years old and healthy.

In the world of gaming, holographic projectors similar to those portrayed on Star Trek came into being and rapidly grew in popularity. They were not quite as sophisticated as the holo-deck on *Star Trek* but were getting closer. Of course, everyone wanted the transporter, but that technology had not yet advanced to the transportation of people. So far, size and complexity were limiting factors; only small objects had been successfully transported over short distances.

Chapter 1 Return to The Island

It had been a couple of days since Captain Walter Phillips, US Marine Corp and his troops stormed the island of Ducie in the South Pacific and secured the suspected compound of Rocky Soto, a terrorist and most wanted criminal by the CIA and FBI. The weather was typical tropical, warm and breezy with an occasional burst of rain. Today was no different from the rest except they were not here to enjoy the tropical beach and sunshine. They had a job to do.

Upon arrival, they experienced no resistance because the island seemed deserted except for birds and the remains of an old military airfield. Captain Phillips and his troops established security and waited for orders as to what to do next. The only information Phillips had received recently had been delivered by Sergeant Blake, the crew chief from the transport that brought them here, which was still sitting on the airfield also waiting for orders.

"Sir, we just received notification that a Colonel Littleton would be arriving shortly; and we are to expect Mr. Josh Randal, Director of CIA and a team to arrive within the week. Our orders are to maintain security and not to turn anything on; just record anything out of the ordinary and to wait," Sergeant Blake reported to his commander.

"Thanks, Blake. Do we have anyone up in that control tower?" Phillips asked.

"Yes, sir."

"Good, make sure nobody turns on anything in any of the labs."

"Yes, sir; I have posted guards on the entrances to the labs and any area with equipment. We did start the generators for power," Blake responded.

"That's fine, maybe we can get some coffee going."

"Already brewing, sir."

After removing all the explosives that the previous owner had left in a failed attempt to destroy the compound, Phillips and his team settled in as security. His troops were instructed to leave everything as it was except the explosives and to not turn anything on.

Colonel Nelson Littleton was a Marine Reservist but was also employed as a senior CIA agent with the team and also had strict orders to leave everything alone. He was six foot three and tipped the scale at just over two hundred and fifteen pounds. Littleton was all Marine, built like a tank, tough and sporting a high and tight haircut typical of Marines, his normally light brown hair looked almost blonde it was so short. Littleton was not part of the initial team, but arrived via a private jet within hours of the island being secured. Contrary to his appearance, he was easy going and very likable.

After stepping off the stairs to his jet, he was confronted by a donkey with a white peacock sitting on its back. They just stood there and eyed each other for a moment before the donkey walked off into the jungle.

"Colonel, I'm Captain Phillips; we did not expect you until tomorrow. Welcome to Ducie Island," Captain Phillips said as he walked up to the Colonel's plane, and saluted. Both of them eyed the donkey as it strolled into the jungle.

"Did you see that?" Littleton asked as he pointed to where the donkey and peacock were standing just a second ago.

"Yes, we have had sightings all over the island; everything from old pilots, Japanese soldiers, donkeys; and, well, the list goes on and on. We have not figured out where they are coming from; they don't say anything; just look at us and then walk away. We believe, and my techs agree, they are holograms and are set just to distract us," Captain Phillips replied.

"Have your men note the time, location and what they see when they are confronted. I don't know, but maybe there is a pattern or they are able to see us too. Technology has become so advanced, I don't believe it is a coincidence," Littleton commented. "Now can we go someplace a bit cooler, standing here in the hot sun is not my idea of fun, unless I have a Margarita in my hand and a beautiful lady under my arm."

"I agree with that sir; I have a vehicle right over here to take us to the compound. It's a short drive," Phillips said and pointed to the waiting driver and Humvee. "We don't have any Margaritas, sorry."

Twenty minutes later, Phillips and Littleton were sitting in a small office discussing what had happened during their arrival and securing of the compound.

"I received word just before I left Peru that Mr. Randal, my boss, will be arriving tomorrow," Littleton stated.

"Didn't expect him until Friday," Phillips commented.

"Plans must have changed since that last report I sent to him. You do know he was seriously injured recently. Maybe the doctors have released him to travel. We shall see tomorrow at any rate," Littleton told Phillips. "Is there any fresh coffee around here?"

"I believe the cook has just made a fresh pot," Phillips commented.

"Good, I need a cup, wish I had a little kicker to put in it," Littleton said as he stood and started for the door.

"Sorry sir, no kicker. We looked at the store room and it was stripped bare. Not so much as a can of beer, and we didn't bring any with us," Phillips said and then added, "Maybe we can have Olson make a goody run back to Peru to pick up some."

"I can't believe you said that Captain; misuse of government equipment could get you years in a small square box," Littleton said with a smile. "But not a bad idea, bet the men would love a cold one after they are off duty, of course. Let me think about it."

Chapter 2 Revealed Secrets

"Colonel, a private jet just requested clearance to land. Should I grant them access?" the young aircraft controller asked over the improvised phone system after finally making contact with the colonel.

The old control tower on the Island had not been used officially for decades. When the Air Force and Marines arrived, they needed to ensure the island remained safe from reporters and anyone else not invited.

"Who's on board?"

"CIA Director Josh Randal and his team, according to the pilot."

"Of course, land them," Colonel Nelson Littleton replied. "I have been expecting him for hours," the colonel said and then slammed the handset down, knocking over the cup of coffee he had been nursing.

Looking around the small office in the compound they had recently secured, he marveled at the technology that the recent occupants had left. True, the place had been wired with explosives that were set to destroy the entire place; but because of reasons unknown to the people that left, the explosives failed to do their job. When the Army arrived, they were able to deactivate all the explosives without incident, saving the compound for analysis.

Forty minutes later, Josh Randal and his team of eight agents walked in the front door of the building in which he and others had been held captive just two weeks earlier. Minutes after entering the room, the door opened again to allow Stephanie Randal to enter; she looked pissed. Rightly so, as she, Josh and several others barely escaped with their lives from this island only now to return to the scene of the crime and attempt to locate the master mind behind the ordeal, Rocky Soto, ex-CIA Research and

Development Director turned terrorist, kidnapper and number one on the FBI most wanted list.

"Nelson, how are you?" Josh said extending his hand to receive his friend's handshake. "I trust you have followed my instructions to secure the compound."

"Yes, sir, all is as requested. This is Captain Phillips; he led the team to secure the compound. He has instructed his techs to not fire up the equipment; and per your orders, we did not. By the way, what is all this stuff?" Colonel Littleton asked holding up a small flat object which looked like a smart phone but he knew it wasn't or at least thought it wasn't.

"Would you have all your troops leave the room for a moment Captain. You may stay, and I will show you," Josh ordered; and when the room was empty, he indicated to his agents to secure the room, lock the door and stand guard. "Nelson what I'm about to show you is straight out of the future and Hollywood would love to have this. This little device is pure twenty-fourth century. It is a little compact hand held programmable holographic generator that would change the gaming world forever and cause real problems for every law enforcement agency on this planet."

Josh took the object from the colonel and pressed the on button located on the side. When the screen came up seconds later, he tapped the screen to activate the program. Within a couple of seconds, Josh was no longer standing in front of the colonel, but instead the President of the United States stood there smiling.

"What the hell, where did Randal go?" Nelson asked looking directly at the President and not believing what he was seeing. And then he looked over at Phillips to see he was shocked at what he was viewing.

"I am still here, gentlemen. This little device is a holographic projector. I can program it to turn me into almost anyone I wish to be, such as now." Josh had not moved, yet standing in front of the them was Bruce Willis complete with bald head and his never-ending smile. Tapping another set of commands, Josh returned to himself once again.

"That is amazing. I can see why you wanted to secure this place. If that got out, who knows what would happen," Colonel Nelson Littleton stated.

"Well, a lot could happen; and a lot has happened including the kidnapping of the President with one of these things. The CIA will release them in the future, but not until we have put in controls to prevent anyone from using them to do bad things. But of course, the best hackers in the world will attempt to break in and use it for whatever they wish. That is why we need a solid encryption system that is uncrackable before we release it," Josh stated. "Okay, you can have your people come back in. We will take up shop in the main control room next door. You and I will maintain this office for now."

"If there is anything you want my troops to do, please let me know," Captain Phillips offered.

"For right now, just keep the place secure. My people are going to need time to download the software and dismantle what we can salvage. We have a ship heading this way to take what we can back to Washington. At some point, I will be opening up the area for your techs to assist in taking down the computers. But not 'til we sanitize them. We cannot let this technology leak out."

"Understood."

"How many troops do you have, Captain?"

"I brought an Army intel unit and my Marine rifle company for security."

"An Intel unit, why?" Randal asked.

"Not really sure; received my orders from command saying to take my rifle company and to have Ft. Bragg supply me with an Intel company with linguists and analysts that have a lot of computer experience. Not sure why, but orders are orders; so I picked up a unit with a variety of linguist and computer geeks.

Sounded strange, but not too much since we were told we were heading to Ducie and the island belonged to Peru."

"Interesting, I didn't request the Intel unit; wonder who added them to the list. I will find out. But since they are here, we can put them to work. Have the intel commander report to me in an hour," Josh requested.

"That would be Captain Banner. I will have him report in an hour. Where? Is there anything else?"

"Mess hall. Yes, one other thing; we will be here for several days, so if you could ensure we have a place to sleep, that would be great. We will eat with you and your troops, if that is okay with you," Josh said. "Oh, the transport at the airfield, have the pilot report to me also. I will need him to assist in transporting some of this out immediately."

"Sure, I will get the First Sergeant to make room in the barracks for you and your people. And I will have Major Olson report to you as soon as we locate her," Phillips answered quickly.

"Thank you," Josh said and then stopped and thought for a second, turning back toward Phillips he said, "Did you say, her?"

"Yes, Major Rhonda Olson is the P.I.C. of the transport. Since arrival and with nothing else to do but relax, she and her crew have been spending a lot of time catching some sun on the beach. I will send someone down to get her."

"Can't say I blame her; this is a beautiful island and that beach did look very inviting. Ask her to meet me here at sixteen hundred. No reason to completely spoil her day at the beach," Josh said. He then looked at his wife and said with a smile, "Did you bring your bikini?"

"Of course, and your thong too," Stephanie teased and followed Josh out of the office and down the hall to the main lab.

Chapter 3 Moving Up

Militia against the Suppressors, MATS, was a small, well organized militia group that needed a new home. It was first formed in the small town of Van Horn, Texas; but the ranch they worked out of was being sold out from under them as renters. They needed a new place to call home. Richard Clark had no idea what to do. His group had grown and most did not want to leave Texas, but he had followers that would go anywhere with him.

MATS was originally set up as a small survival training center but grew into something larger and more sinister. Suppression of the Constitution, suppression against human rights, suppression of free speech, the right to own weapons to protect themselves were just some of what they are going against the government for. The original charter of the training facility was to train people in the art of survival. Once the candidate completed the course, they were asked, innocently, to join MATS. After more indoctrination and training, each member became more and more involved. What started as a small group of eleven grew to a militia of over eighty during their ten-year period of growth.

Richard Clark was sitting in a local café having lunch in downtown Van Horn, Texas when he was approached by a short, stocky, oriental man dressed in a custom tailored grey suit. The man stood about five foot six, bald on the top with grey hair sticking out around his ears. He sported a pair of horn rim glasses, white shirt and blue tie. He wore cowboy boots that were scuffed and dirty, contrary to the crisp suit. He sat down across from Richard and just stared at him for a moment.

"Okay, you called me; what is it you want?" Clark asked quietly between bites of his hamburger.

"Mr. Clark, I have a proposition for you, but you are not to tell anyone that you ever met me or mention anything about this offer. Do you understand? Failure to comply will result in very dire circumstances for you and your little group," the oriental said with a slight oriental accent.

"I understand, but understand me. If this is some kind of bull shit scam, I will hunt you down; and when they find all the pieces, they may be able to put you back together, but I really don't believe they will," Richard agreed. He was a man of statue, over six foot four, broad shouldered, square jawed and with long brown hair tied into a ponytail. Richard almost always wore old faded combat fatigue pants, a brown tee shirt, vest and desert combat boots. He never left home without his best friend, a Colt Python 44 magnum revolver in a worn leather holster strapped to his hip.

"Not a scam. An honest up front offer to help you build everything you want, but I will need you to do some jobs for me, without question and when I tell you."

"What's your offer, Mr. ah, I don't know your name?" Clark said.

"My name is unimportant and you will never see me again. I plan on sending you a quarter of million dollars every month for the next four months. At the end of that time, you will have established your organization and completed the few jobs I have for you. I will initially give you five million dollars in three days, and you are to move your group to North Dakota. There is a new facility there that you will take over and continue to grow and train. Do you agree?"

"That's an offer that only a fool would refuse. I agree," Clark said and held out his hand to shake on the deal. "Before I forget, what kind of jobs do you want us to complete? Who owns this place in North Dakota?"

"Today, I will give you a hundred thousand dollars, directions to the compound, and my direct secure phone number. Do not give it to anyone other than your second in command," the oriental said.

"When do I find out about these jobs you want us to do?" Clark asked.

"You will be told in sufficient time to prepare for what I need," he said and then handed Clark an envelope containing some cash, a cell phone number, and the directions to the compound in North Dakota, ignoring his question. "I will be in contact," he said and then stood and walked out of the café.

Twenty minutes later, Clark paid his bill and walked out of the café. He paused for a moment to look up and down the street for the old man. Not seeing him, he climbed into his Ford Bronco and backed out into the street.

After arriving at the ranch, he gathered his men and laid out the plan. Half of them said they had families in Van Horn and did not want to leave. Several more had decided that being in a militia was not something they really wanted to do anymore, saying they needed to work to support their families and declined on moving to North Dakota. This brought Clark's team down to twenty-five total including himself. He thanked the men and women that had supported his movement, and allowed them to leave without question. He was sorry to see some very good people leave, but he understood their situation and would not hold it against them. The remaining members made plans to move to North Dakota within the week.

Chapter 4 Infiltration

Deep in the back country of North Dakota near the small town of Devil's Lake, a large ex-missile site was located which was now dedicated to recruiting and training the militia group known as 'MATS'. The missile site had been deactivated years earlier and sold. The new owner spent millions renovating, updating systems and with the help of the government added some new equipment for defense. The new occupants had no idea what they had taken by force. Only a few people knew what was buried underground and they were not talking.

It was early August, four months after Clark had brought his militia to the missile site and forced his way in. With the assistance of the local police chief and a couple of crooked judges, they were able to remove all the resident workers, telling them they had to leave or be arrested for trespassing. The local police chief served illegal documents condemning the site and gave the site to Clark.

Davin and Connie Pierce were standing at the gate wearing ragged jeans, tee shirts, baseball caps and not in disguise as Kelly Donavan and his wife but as Davin and Connie Pierce waiting for someone to come and allow them to enter the compound. They had been waiting for forty minutes since they walked up to the gate and pushed the button marked 'For Assistance' and spoken with the voice that responded. Looking past the gate, they could not see any buildings, just open range with a few cows wandering aimlessly while eating the sparse grass that was available.

The morning was warm for this time of year, but they knew that soon the weather would turn white and very cold. North Dakota had harsh winters and they did not want to be caught outside for that first snow fall.

"Is this going to work, Davin?" Connie asked looking very worried.

"It has to," Davin replied, "It has to."

"Look someone is coming," she said pointing toward a truck racing toward them on the dirt road, throwing up a lot of dust.

"It's show time," Davin stated.

Minutes later, the rusted and badly dented pickup truck skidded to a stop in a cloud of dirt and dust. One man and a woman stepped out and looked at their new guests. Both were dressed in desert camouflage pants and brown tee-shirts, the standard issue uniform for militia members. Both also had, strapped to their legs, holsters which carried a semi-automatic pistol. Davin and Connie could not determine the type or size but assumed they were at least nine millimeters, standard military issue, and the chosen weapon of many militia and military. However, the US Army and Marines had actually switched back to the more powerful and trusted forty-five caliber pistol a couple of decades ago.

"How can we help you two?" the woman asked as they walked up to the gate.

"We want to join your cause," Connie replied to her.

"What are your qualifications? We are an elite group, and you have to have something to offer?" the woman replied.

"I, ah," Connie started but was cut off when the woman raised her hand for her to stop talking.

"No, him," she replied while pointing at Davin. "Does the old man speak?"

"Yes I speak; I was just being polite. Without going into a lot of detail out here in the middle of nowhere, I bring more to the table than you can imagine."

"Oh, I can imagine a lot, Mr. Pierce."

"You know who we are?"

"Yes, of course we do. Why do you think it took us so long to get out here? We were doing a background check on you two. Ex CIA and FBI, impressive, wanted for murder and escaping from jail."

"Well, the murder yes; but I never broke out of jail because I was never in jail," Davin responded.

"Yeah, there is that; how did you pull that off? No wait, come on, get in the truck; we can discuss this with the boss," she said and signaled for her male friend to open the gate.

Davin looked at Connie and smiled, step one complete. They had passed through the gate, and were inside the compound. Now all they had to do was to find Brian Forest and stop whatever they were planning. That should be easy, since he was the Boss, as they called him.

The ride in the truck bed was rough and dusty, lasting ten minutes of hell. At least they had thrown in a couple of cushions to sit on.

Davin and Connie had been on the run for a couple of months, dodging the police and the FBI, when they finally received orders from Josh Randal to infiltrate the compound and get Brian and his partner out. So they had headed for North Dakota to attempt to get into a militia group that had been growing over the past few months. Although MATS had managed to stay out of the news, they had attracted the attention of the FBI, especially since the President's half-brother, Brain Forest, was an undercover Secret Service agent and presently leading the militia group.

Davin sat in the back of that old truck with only one thought on his mind, *'I am getting too old for this shit.'*

President Tony Sanford had been in contact with Brian on a weekly basis and was recently told that they were planning something big, which he was attempting to stop but was being out maneuvered by his second in command, George 'Moose' Monahan. Davin and Connie were tasked to go in to assist Brian and to find out who was supplying the funding and weapons for this group and to stop Monahan from whatever he was planning.

If all went well, they would be out of the cold north by the end of the month, long before the snow started to fall. But as everyone knows, the best laid plans do not always go as planned.

Chapter 5 How Deep Is Deep?

"Josh, are they in?" Tony Sanford asked of his friend and CIA Director.

"Yes, and their cover is as tight as we can make it," Josh replied and then took a sip of his coffee.

"Any word on Rocky Soto?" Tony asked changing the subject.

"We had a lead that he was seen in Tahiti, but this guy is slippery. He disappeared right in front of our agent."

"Was he possibly using his holograph technology?" "That is the only way he could just disappear, but we are not completely sure it was really him. Remember there are a lot of Orientals in the islands; and without stereo typing, a lot do look alike especially from a distance," Josh confided, not really wanting to say that; but it was true, and that made his job much harder.

"Okay, Korea has been up in arms about some videos of the Prime Minister and some of his closest political figures in compromising positions with minors, same sex encounters and prostitutes. What have you heard about those?" Tony asked.

"They seem to be amateur videos that are being broadcast over different television stations and the web; they seem to be using Facebook, Instagram and Twitter to their advantage. We believe that Soto has something to do with it, using his holographic programs to make them. But, of course, it could be their own people trying to discredit the PM. Why? We don't know; maybe just to piss off the powers over there. China is up in arms because Korea is blaming them. To the point Korea attacked and nearly sank one of China's frigates. We have learned that there are at least forty-six killed and many injured. Now China is mobilizing their military; could lead to war over there, dragging Japan and most likely us into the conflict. We, of course, don't need another war," Josh explained as he described what he knew about the situation.

"That is so true, Josh. We don't need another war. I will send a message to both and ask for a truce and a meeting on neutral ground to nip this in the bud as it were," Tony suggested and then took a deep breath. "Seems like we are always trying to stop a war or send troops into a war zone, when we should be taking care of everyone at home. We spend millions on other countries which we could use fixing our own country."

"That may work; doing nothing is not an option. But don't drag us into war, old man," Josh stated quietly. After a pause, he continued, "I agree, we need to spend more on the home front. But being the most powerful nation on the planet has its drawbacks." Josh waited for a comment from the President; and after not getting one, he continued, "Let's get back to our old friend Soto. We have had some traffic indicating he is working with some very well backed Middle Eastern terrorist groups, the remnants of ISIS. We have not confirmed it yet; but believe he is also supporting the MATS group up in North Dakota. Davin and Connie are in, but I have not heard from them since they entered the compound," Josh commented restarting the conversation on the MATS group.

"ISIS, they have been quiet for a while; thought we eliminated them completely in 2018. What makes you think they are involved? When is Davin supposed to report?" Sanford asked.

"When he gets clear, so that is up for grabs, sir. We have an open channel to them; and when they get a free chance, they will call us. Your brother and his partner are there and should be able to work it so they will have some time alone. That's if his cover isn't blown and he is still alive. When was the last you heard from him?"

"It's been over a week. The compound is pretty tight and most of it is in a blind spot for cell phones, so the use of a sat phone is required and you know as well as I do that those have their own problems in certain areas. And they picked the right spot to limit communications in and out of the compound," Sanford stated. "Tell me more about the ISIS connection."

"Not much to tell. They have been quiet for several years, but we have been getting intel that they are looking to buy more weapons to include a WMD," Josh commented, referencing weapons of mass destruction.

"We can't have that! And you think Soto is working with them to get a WMD?" Sanford questioned.

"Yes. I will provide you with more information as we get it; we have operatives on the inside. With any luck, we will know who and when; and if they get what they want, have time to take them out before getting the use of their purchases," Josh said with a smile.

"Okay, what about the compound in North Dakota? Tell me more about it," Sanford asked.

"We moved a satellite to monitor the compound; and even with a stationary satellite, we have not been able to see much, Josh continued. The site is an old Sprint Missile facility. Most everything was built underground and is nuclear hardened; so unless they are playing on the surface, we have little to no intel. We did try infrared, but because of the depth of the site that was a futile effort; but we had to try. There is also some kind of electronic interference around the area which is preventing us from using our long range listening equipment," Josh commented and then added, "We have intercepted communications between several high ranking ISIS leaders and Soto. They are coded, but we broke the code; it seems they are exchanging technology and funds to build something. As of yet, we don't know what that something is, but we are working on it. Does Brian know about the defense system we have there?"

"That blows, so we have sent in two, no four operatives into a situation completely blind?" the President asked, "And, yes, Brian and his partner, Mona, know about the system."

"That is why we suspect Soto being involved; he has the knowledge and resources to create a lot of high tech gadgetry, including an electronic shield to prevent our satellites from seeing or hearing anything from them," Josh reported.

"We need to stop this guy and end this ISIS now. Any idea of where he is?"

"If we knew that, sir, we would have taken him down already. However, we are getting closer every day. Did your brother give you any indication as to what is going on there?" Stephanie asked.

"He didn't say much, afraid of getting caught," Sanford replied.

"Maybe since he now has assistance, they will be able to uncover who is supporting them; and if it is Soto, then we can finally nail him," Josh said smiling. He was worried; Davin and Connie had not done any undercover work in years. He hoped they were up to the challenge and survived.

Chapter 6 Sprint Missile Base

The truck stopped in front of a small ranch house in a cloud of dust and dirt. Davin and Connie looked around and saw only the ranch house, a barn in very bad shape and a very old John Deer Tractor sitting with its front axle on blocks.

"Wow, is this a militia compound or a rundown ranch?" Connie asked.

"I believe the rundown ranch, seems to qualify for government aid and soon," Davin commented.

"Come with me," the female said when she stepped out of the cab and started to walk to the front door with Davin and Connie right behind her. The driver engaged the transmission, drove the truck over to the barn, and disappeared inside.

After stopping at the door, she turned toward them and said, "You're going to meet with Brian; he is in charge, and he will decide if you get to stay, taken back out to the road or buried on the ridge over there. So be respectful, Mr. Pierce, the ice you two are walking on is very thin. We know who you are and what you had supposedly done. All of which could be fabricated," she said and then opened the door.

"Wait a second, Miss. We came here because the feds are out for blood, ours. If you don't want us here, then get that truck back here right now and take us back to the road. We will do our best out there without your help."

"Not my decision, Pierce. Brian will decide. Now, let's go in, and you can convince him. But he is very skeptical about any outsiders. Just so you, know, I will let him tell you. Are you ready?"

"Let's go," Davin said.

After opening the door, she let them pass her into a large open area that probably was the living room. But this one was pretty empty; there was only a sofa, coffee table, two lamps and a beat up leather lounge chair; no TV or stereo could be seen anywhere in the room.

"Come, I am in the kitchen. Please come on back," a voice yelled from the back of the house.

"Through there," she said as she pointed toward the door on the other side of the room, turned, and left the house.

Davin and Connie looked at each other and then at the back of the woman that just left the house. They shrugged, turned, walked to the door, and entered a brightly lit kitchen where a tall dark haired man with a full beard in jeans and light green tee shirt was leaning over the stove cooking something that smelled extremely good.

"What are you cooking?" Connie asked the dark haired man as they entered the kitchen. He was standing by the stove stirring something in a large Dutch oven. Looking closer, they noticed he had a short beard that was showing signs of gray and tan or rather dirty cowboy boots. They stopped short of the table when they heard a low growl and saw a large German Shepherd in the corner of the room. The growl caused both of them to come to a halt not knowing if they were going to be attacked.

"Chili, my mom's recipe," came the reply without anyone looking over at who had entered the kitchen, "And that is Chilly on the floor; don't mind her, more of a pussy cat than a guard dog, well until told it is guard time, then watch your step. Please help yourself to a drink; there are beers and sodas in the fridge."

"Thanks, would love a cold beer," Davin said, "Connie what would you like?"

"Beer is good for me too, thanks," she replied and walked over to where Chilly was lying and petted her, "She's awesome. How old is she?"

Davin retrieved a couple of beers, paused, and looked at the cook as he held up a beer for him and received a nod in acceptance.

"Thanks, take a seat, I am almost done. She is going on two, and has been with me since birth. Faithful and loyal, the best dog I have ever had," the cook said as he stirred the chili.

"Who do we have the honor of having a beer with?" Davin asked as he and Connie sat at the large kitchen table.

"Oh, sorry, I am Brian Forest, unelected commander, leader, general do all, boss of bosses of this undefined palace."

"Okay you are in charge, but this looks like a rundown ranch, not anything we need to worry about, or are we gravely mistaken?"

"No, it is a rundown ranch; but we do have some stuff, and a couple of people living here, whom you may or may not meet soon. That will depend on you, and, of course, my decision," Brian said and then accepted the beer when it was handed to him.

"Okay, what do we have to do to get admittance to your ranch?" Connie asked between sips of beer. "Damn, this beer surely tastes great after that dusty ride in your pickup."

Brian walked over to the table, pulled out a chair, sat across from Davin and Connie, and then stated, "This room has no bugs, except a few cockroaches and ants during the summer and some fleas on Chilly. So we can talk freely in here." He stuck out his hand to receive Davin's handshake. "I know why you are here and why I am here, but my brother doesn't understand the importance of my mission. I hope you do."

"We were not told a lot except to come here and get you and your partner out as quickly as possible. He did not say why," Davin said between sips of beer.

"Okay, we will depart in a couple of days. First, I need to show you what is here and introduce you to my other partner. Chilly is my lifetime partner," Brian said and then signaled for Chilly to come over to him.

She stood up, walked over to Brian, sat beside him, and looked up until she received a pat on her head. "We have a lot to talk about and a few things that have to be done before any of us get to leave. First, and foremost, there is George 'Moose' Monahan. You will meet him soon enough. Yes, I am in charge here, by default;

but Moose is attempting to take over, and in a few words, he has already threatened me. When we go down below, I will give you the whole story and much more. Even though this room is not bugged, we cannot discuss everything here."

Chapter 7 South Pacific

Rocky Soto was having dinner with his son at their new home. It was located on the beach on the northwest side of the island of Tahiti. They had recently purchased the home from the local bank when he and his crew decided it was the best place to lay low and enjoy the sights and sounds of the South Pacific. The weather was great; the food out of this world; and as long as he and his crew didn't attract attention, they would be fine for months. The view from the patio where they sat was overlooking the beach and they could see the harbor a mile away. All was as it should be, quiet, beautiful and safe, at least for now.

"Father, how long are we going to stay here?" Horatio asked as he spooned some soup into his mouth, dripping some down his chin.

"Not much longer. We will keep the house, but will need to move after we start the next phase," Rocky stated and then took a large piece of lobster and dipped it in some butter sauce.

"Where are we going?"

"Not far, but I need to start the next phase away from our home and then most likely return here and fade into the sunset, as they say."

"Good, I met a girl yesterday and would love to get to know her better," Horatio said with a smile.

"You don't have to go; if you want to fade into the night, I can do this on my own."

"Really, dad, I thought you needed me. I'm hurt." He attempted to look hurt, but he was not hurt at all; he was just hoping that his dad would not see that he had other plans.

"Yes, I need you; but if we, I mean, I get caught, you will not be dragged down with me. Maybe it would be a good idea if you did bow out. Get comfortable with your girl and give me some grandkids," Soto commented, smiling.

"Maybe that is a good idea. I will sleep on it, okay," Horatio agreed and then said quietly, "I am meeting with Tara tonight; can I use the car."

"Sure, I will be on the computer tonight," Rocky said with a smile. "I need to set up a few things with our people and have our pilot prep the jet. So go out and enjoy."

"Would you like to meet Tara, she is Japanese and, well, you can judge for yourself when you meet her."

"Why not bring her by before you go out on the town," Rocky suggested.

"Okay, how about five, and then we can head out to dinner and a movie," Horatio agreed smiling.

"Good; looking forward to meeting her." Rocky replied, paused for a second, and then asked, "What's her name?" After another pause, he thought and then said, "Oh, no, wait, tonight is not good for me, maybe some other time. I just remembered I need to meet with my ship's captain before he sails in the morning."

"Oh, Tara, Tara Wong, she is very beautiful. I think you will like her. I will bring her around some other time and you can meet."

"Good, Wong is a strong name in our country; she must come from a strong honorable blood line. Is she related to Benjamin Wong by any chance?"

"I really don't know, father," Horatio answered curious as to why his father was asking. "Who is Benjamin Wong?"

"An old family friend, haven't seen him in years; we attended the same High School. Last I heard, he was CEO of some big computer company in Los Angeles. I was just curious if he had spun off a daughter. Ben was kind of a lady's man; maybe he finally settled down and well…" Rocky said, and let his words fade off as he looked at his son. "She must be very special, I would love to meet her, but we may not have time. You spend some time with her; I have work to do."

Chapter 8 Ranch House Chili

"Davin and Connie, I know why you are here and am sure my brother has good intentions. After you finish your beer, grab a couple more and let's take a walk," Brian said. He stood up and stirred his chili again, placed a lid on the pot and turned down the heat.

"Before we leave, can you tell us why we are here?" Connie asked and then took a big sip of beer finishing the bottle. She stood up and retrieved three more, looking down at the sleeping Chilly.

"You are here because I need your help; the people financing this place have some very dangerous plans, mainly to destroy the United States. Your boss and my brother think they know who it is; and are hoping, by having you here, it will attract him here so we can arrest him. But the intel they have received is not conclusive, Rocky Soto may be behind this, but where the hell did he get all the money? My personal belief is the money is from ISIS, or some other well-funded terrorist group. Someone is backing him, so we need to follow the money to the source, where ever it takes us."

"Okay, let's go," Davin said as he stood to leave.
"Out the back door, this way," Brian said as he opened the back door and exited onto a large porch with a swing on one end and several potted plants.

"Great view! Would be a nice place to relax and drink," Davin commented as they followed Brian down the steps and into the back yard. Connie looked over her shoulder to see that Chilly was close behind.

"Usually I am in that swing over there with a cold one and enjoying the sunset, but we can do that later; for now, follow me and I will explain as we go along," Brian stated, "This place is a decommissioned Sprint Missile Base. It was used until the end of the Cold War. Henry L. Rothschild purchased it as an investment; his plan was to provide a home for veterans that were in need. He is a retired Congressman from the great state of North Freezing Dakota. He owned a construction company and brought them in to convert the facility into a hospital and barracks to house the staff. Doctors and nurses were to be hired and moved out here after construction was complete. Keeping all the work in house and with a little assistance from our government, he was able to finish the place in record time and include some very up-to-date equipment."

"You said he finished in record time. So, where are the buildings, what happened?" Davin enquired as they looked around.

"You are standing on them. Because of the severe weather we have up here in North Dakota, everything was built underground; and, of course, being a secret, sort of, missile base, the entire facility is directly under our feet. When reconstruction and modifications were completed about a year ago, we had a two hundred bed hospital, barracks to house a staff of a hundred complete with dining facilities, game rooms, and much more. The facility had sat empty since the end of the Cold War and its decommissioning, but then purchased and converted."

"Okay, can we see it?" Connie asked looking for an entrance.

"I will take you in shortly. But I need to explain what happened, so bear with me," Brian continued. He stopped and reached down to look Chilly in the eye; she had followed Brian out the back door. He gave Chilly a silent command. Chilly immediately turned and ran toward the barn and disappeared inside. After standing, Brian continued, "Everything was built, equipment and supplies trucked and or flown in. We do have an airport, long runway, paved and lighted but well hidden under the lake over there," he said pointing to a lake about three hundred yards beyond the barn. "We drain the lake when we need to use it. Everything was falling into place; staff were hired and moved into the barracks, not a full staff but enough to get started. Great idea, but then Henry woke up dead one morning. Our newly hired doctor said it was natural causes, but I don't believe it. He wasn't sick; had no signs of illness. But the doc said heart attack. That's when Richard Clark took over and things started to change. He brought in mercenaries, supposedly to protect the place, and converted one of the storage bays in the barracks into a weapons range. A large group of mercs moved in within weeks of him taking over. He told us what his plan was, which was completely different from Henry's. I was his lieutenant and tried to convince him that what he was doing was wrong. He wanted his militia and he told me in no way was he going to let a lowly lieutenant tell him what to do; and he wanted to change the way the United States was doing business, by force if necessary. I did not know at the time, but he had his group from Texas move in; his plan all along was to take over from Henry, which leads me to believe he killed Henry. He said if I didn't cooperate he would make sure I ended up on the ridge beside Henry."

"Wow, where is Clark now?" Davin asked.
"He is buried next to Henry over there in the cemetery," Brian said pointing toward the hill over to the east of the property.

"That put you in charge. How did he die?" Connie asked, letting her FBI background come to the surface. "And may I ask, what did you tell Chilly to do?"

"You will understand soon; we will talk about Clark later. Right now, you need to understand that I am attempting to complete what Henry started. I have ordered the mercenaries that are here to leave, but they are not leaving; and rumor has it that they are planning to kill me and take over. Some left when I said there was no more money to buy food or weapons. I lied, of course. Some believed me, others did not; my days are numbered, and it is not a high number. I have been lucky and am still here. This is where you and Connie come in; you need to help me stay alive, and get rid of the mercenaries. I have asked my brother to make sure we are not bothered until I call for the Calvary; he said he would try, but if it came down to sending in the troops and rescuing me, us, then he would send them."

"How many are there?" Davin asked. "And are you the only operative here?"

"Forty-one, led by an ex-Marine by the name of George Monahan, nickname 'Moose'. I mentioned him earlier. Big guy, tips the scale at around two fifty, all muscle. He was a Captain in the Marines before getting kicked out for striking a superior officer. He became a mercenary, working for anyone with money enough to pay him and his buddies. He does listen to me because, and only because, Clark had named me as his lieutenant and to succeed him if he was not around or killed." After pausing for a moment, he added, "They have weapons and training; they are looking for more of their kind and want to make this a training base. I can't let that happen."

"Where are they now?" Davin asked still a bit confused as to what was going on.

"You met two of them earlier. That was Sonja and Max the Mouse. They usually just patrol the ranch and do odd jobs for me and Moose. You may have noticed they were both armed, but not dangerous; they just act like they are big shots."

"What about the rest of them?"
"Most are traveling right now, recruiting as it were. That leaves Moose and fifteen of his team here. Well, counting Sonja and Max there are eighteen here; and the rest gone for now."

"Where is the entrance, Brian? And, where is your partner?"

"The entrance is through the storm cellar under the ranch house, where else would it be?" Brian said and then turned and started to walk back toward the house. "I need to check the chili and then we go seventy feet down. Yes, I have a partner here, never work alone; you met Chilly, she is my partner and will be until the end. As for a human partner, you will meet her soon."

"What about Chilly?" Connie asked. "Where did she go?"

"She will catch up shortly," Brian said.

Chapter 9 Paradise

Sunday morning sunrise on Tahiti was like a new beginning for those that lived and partied there. The people of the island started to rise; some had been up for hours getting their resorts ready for new guests and for the ones that had been there for a while. Scuba instructors were preparing their equipment for early morning dives, bartenders were restocking their bars, maids and hotel employees were busy opening umbrellas on the beach, sweeping out the evening trash and generally getting ready for another day in paradise.

Rocky Soto was up early and working on his computer. He had a lot to organize before he had to catch the shuttle to the international airport. He was to meet the captain of his ship at the airport and they had a flight to Hong Kong, where he would meet up with his ship and crew. His engineers had been updating the software on their equipment and adding new gadgets to improve on the technology they had already. With the new software, they should be able to complete their mission. He was worried; the Beta testing in the lab and all the simulations showed him that he was on the right track. However, lab tests and reality were sometimes not quite the same. Too many factors to put into the equation, too many things that could go wrong, and as the old saying by that fictional guy Murphy, 'If it aint' broke, don't fix it'. No that's not it, 'The best laid battle plan goes to hell when the shooting starts,' no that's not it either, oh yeah, this one, 'If everything seems to be going well, you have obviously overlooked something.' Yeah that one, old Murphy had a way of jumping in when you least expect him. And right now everything was going along as planned. Rocky thought about it for a while and decided he had everything in order and that nothing was left out. Thinking of old Murphy's Laws made him smile, because he knew he did not leave anything to chance; he and his team had thought of everything that could possibly go wrong, or did he?

Rocky checked in Horatio's room and discovered his son had not returned home all night. He thought that someday he might have grandchildren and that Horatio was with his girl. That was a good thing, by keeping him out of all this, his son would likely have a good long safe life. This next phase of the project was going to be very dangerous; and he did not want his son dead, at least not yet.

Eight hours later, Soto was walking up the gang plank with his captain to meet with the crew and check on the status of his next big adventure. With the upgrades to the software and new equipment installed on board his ship, getting to his objective should not be a problem. The only unknown factor was the weather. The weather on the open ocean can sometimes cause havoc to the best laid plans. According to the National Weather Forecast, he would have clear sailing for the next twenty days, more than enough time to complete this phase.

Failing to get China and North Korea into a shooting war was not a problem, but failing to bring the President of the United States and the CIA Director down was a big problem. The holographic videos of high-ranking members of the Chinese and North Korean parties with under-aged prostitutes and members of the same sex did not prove productive, but were fun making and broadcasting. Smiling as he walked up the gangway, he was thinking about those as well as some other movies, how inflammatory they were, and the role they played in his success to bring down the Assistant CIA Director. Life was good and his technology was making it very interesting for the world. But they had not seen anything yet, phase four of his plan would create more deceit and hatred around the world.

"Welcome aboard Rocky," the *Bonaventure* Captain said as they stepped onto the deck.

"Thank you, Captain." Soto replied and then directed his attention to the tall man dressed in a white navy uniform standing at attention at the top of the gangway and asked, "Are my techs in the lab?"

"Yes, and they are really happy you are here now; they have a lot to show you. I have to get back to the bridge, unless you want to delay departure," the young man stated and started toward the bridge. "Captain, we are running late, and you are also needed on the bridge."

"No, let's get going, we need to be on site by noon on May 21st. Any problem with that?" Soto asked.

"No, sir, we will be under way in an hour. Except we still have crew onshore," the young man replied, "Do you wish to delay leaving until they arrive?" Getting a no for an answer, the Captain and young man turned and headed for the bridge while Soto turned and walked to the lab located two decks below the main deck.

"I'm going to the lab and find out what is going on," Rocky said and thought about Murphy's laws again. "Captain, prepare the ship for departure; we leave in two hours with or without the missing crew."

Chapter 10 Seventy Feet Below

Brian walked over to the back of the ranch house and pulled open the storm cellar door to expose a pair of heavy blast doors. He moved the handle to open the door to show a lighted stairway that looked like any other stairwell going down into a storm cellar.

Starting down the steps with Davin and Connie close behind, they reached a small landing with two elevator doors. Brian walked over to the panel on the door, inserted a key card, and then pressed the down button on the left set of doors. He then reached over and pressed another button and the blast doors started to close behind them.

He turned and smiled at his two visitors and said quietly, "What you are about to see is something right out of Hollywood, at least our version of Hollywood. Both elevators go to the basement, and give you access to most of the facility. We do have other entrances located around the compound, where the elevators come to the surface, one is in the barn to load and unload medical patients that are on stretchers or wheelchairs," Brian said as he entered the elevator and pushed the B6 button and watched as the doors closed. "Located in the ranch house and the barn are air circulation systems to keep the facility cool in the summer and heated during our extreme winters. Even at seventy feet below the surface, it can get very cold. We had to hide most of the above ground structures; the barn and ranch house are the main structures that were either added or converted to look like they do now. Seventy feet below the surface is level one; there are six levels going as deep as two hundred feet below the surface. We will go all the way down and then come back up to level three and start the tour. I want to show you the lowest level first, because it is where the additional generators, air scrubbers and supplies are stored."

"I thought the CIA had some cool facilities, but this beats that hands down," Connie commented and then stood awestruck as the doors opened to expose a long lighted hallway that was void of any life. "Where is everyone?"

"As I said upstairs, most are out recruiting and those that are here have jobs around the ranch to keep up the appearance that we are a working, albeit broke ranch. And this level and all levels below three are off limits to everyone except me, Mona and a few select trusted assistants of mine. This is level four." Brian paused, stepped into the hall, waved them to follow, and continued, "As I said upstairs, this was a missile site; it had twelve missile silos which have been converted to apartments. You will be getting your own floor, complete with its own bathroom, living room, and bedroom. We have 4,000 square feet in the ranch house and over 12,000 square feet underground. The original building that is now inside of the ranch house was 2,400 square feet. We had to add to it to ensure that it looked like a ranch house and not a military compound."

"The doors on this hall are the hospital wards for patients that are able to walk. The hall to the left is for patients that are unable to move under their own power and the one to the right is the ICU. The three floors above us are identical to this one. All patient floors are set up with private rooms or rooms for two. The rooms on level one are a little plusher for VIP guests. Feel free to open any door and look, your room will be on level two. We have no patients right now and probably will not until we get things back in order. We do have a small medical staff which usually can be found in one of the recreation rooms. They have limited duties right now, since we have no guests needing medical attention," Brian said and continued down the hall, stopping in front of a pair of double doors marked surgery. "This is one of our fully equipped surgery facilities and recovery area; on level one, this same room is the gym and recreation room; on level two it is another full surgery facility and recovery area."

"This is amazing; how did you get it built without anyone noticing?" Connie asked.

"Easy, we are so far away from city lights and no satellites passed over this area for many years. This facility was completed in the early sixties, and we just modified it to meet our needs. So there really wasn't any construction except for the modifications to the existing buildings and the construction of a barn which houses the vehicles, medical elevator, generators and ventilation systems. We modified it a bit to handle the construction. It took two years to modify."

"What did this cost? And where are the construction workers that built it?"

"I have no idea how much it cost to purchase and remodel this place; I didn't pay for it. The original builders were of course the U.S. government. As for the workers; they probably died years ago, and if not, they still are under secrecy laws they agreed to when they built the original missile site. I do know that when the government built it as a Sprint Missile site, they spent over three million in 1960's dollars. On a side note, just for fun I did use standard government forms which I downloaded from the Internet to get the things you can't buy on the local market and to have the workers sign non-disclosure forms used by the government to cover our butts. Rothchild paid for the modifications and died before it was completed. We told the contractors that this was going to be a super-secret facility and they understood what would happen," Brian explained. "Just like the government does when they build a SCIF and when they originally built this place. We just made it better and looking like a ranch instead of a missile site. And, yeah, the locals know it is here, but don't know what it is being used for now."

"Now that is pretty cool; we have a super-secret facility located in North Dakota, paid for by some guy named Rothchild, and not operated by our government. It is run by a bunch of mercenaries, present company excused of course," Davin commented as he looked in at the surgery/operating room. "The agency could surely use this place. A very secure safe house for our operatives, I mean their operatives."

"Yeah, would be cool. This place reminds me of that old TV show '*Agents of Shield*' having a secret underground facility and a lot of high tech gadgets. By the way, where are all the high tech gadgets?" Connie asked; she stopped when they reached the cross roads of the two halls and turned around, looked down each hall and was unsure of what she was seeing.

"What's wrong Connie?" Brian asked when he saw she wasn't walking anymore.

"I just have a bad feeling about all this. You don't know who is paying for all this, right. Rothschild is dead; did he leave a will or any money to pay for this?"

"He is dead and buried, his will left his entire fortune to the facility and it is all gone. It took all of it to almost pay for the reconstruction, when it ran out there was still about two hundred thousand that wasn't paid. But then suddenly money started to show up, cash money. I immediately paid off the balance of the debt and stockpiled the rest of the money as it came in. It has been delivered by FedEx once every month for the past four months. Each package contained a quarter of million dollars, old bills, not sequential or counterfeit."

"This is just getting better by the minute," Davin said and then opened a door to find a young lady watching the television. "Oh, sorry, didn't know this room was occupied."

"That's okay, I was just taking a break. Is Brian with you?" she asked.

"Yes, do you need to talk to him?" Davin replied.

"No, not now, but tell him to stop by at seven, if he wants to see his favorite show on the big screen. I will be in the theater," she said, then looked down at her feet and stroked Chilly on the head and quietly stated, "Brian's here." Chilly stood, picked up a small package that was on the floor inches from her nose and immediately walked out of the room and up to Brian giving him the package.

"Okay, theater at seven," Davin repeated and then closed the door. "Did you hear?" looking at Brian.

"Yeah, that's Mona; she is my girlfriend and partner. We like to watch NCIS on Tuesday night. And before you ask, we do have a theater with a one hundred and twenty-inch screen and get to watch television on it along with movies. Pretty neat system. If you want to join us tonight, the theater is upstairs one level, take the elevator or the stairs at the end of each hall." Then Brian reached down and patted Chilly on the head and she dropped a small item into his hand. "Thanks Chilly, now let's go to the armory."

"Popcorn?" Davin asked.

"Of course, with butter, now let's go upstairs and get a room for you two," Brian stated and headed for the stairs. "But we have another stop before I take you to your room."

"Where's that?" Connie asked as she followed.

"Armory, we need to get you two armed. Unless you are already armed?" Brian said as he opened the door to the stairs, and slipped the package into his pocket. "Let's go Chilly." They started down the hallway.

Chapter 11 Old School Intelligence

"Good morning, Josh," Meredith Brown said when she saw her boss walk into the office.

"Morning, Miss Brown," Josh replied and continued past her and entered his office. He closed the door behind him. Meredith looked up confused; he had not acted like that ever, at least as far as she knew. Something was very wrong; and she, being his personal secretary and friend, wanted to help, but knew that she should not interfere until asked. She wasn't built that way. She stood, walked over to the credenza, poured herself a cup of coffee, and waited patiently. Josh would come out and tell her what was going on when he was ready.

Josh stepped behind his desk and sat down. He placed his hands over his face, leaned forward, put his elbows on his desk, and tried to gather himself; he was worried, extremely worried. His best friend had just walked into Dante's Inferno and he had no contact with him. He looked at the phone and was tempted to call the President and request permission to send in a team to rescue his friend and the President's brother.

He knew he could not do that; this was an undercover operation based on old school tradecraft. This meant that there was no assistance from any of the high tech gadgets that were at the disposal of most agents. Additionally, Davin and Connie were not young strong field operatives; they were seasoned, but had been out of the field for years. Could they pull this off without getting killed?

The phone on his desk rang disturbing his concentration and quiet. He hesitated to answer letting it ring five times before picking the handset up and saying, "Josh Randal, what can I do for the President today?"

"Josh, I just received a coded message from Brian and wanted you to know that your people have entered the compound and have made contact with him," Tony Sanford said quickly.

"Good, anything else?"

"Yes, but it was a bit cryptic. He said, and I quote, 'things are not what they seem'."

"What did he mean by that?" Josh asked.

"I don't know but have a team assembled and ready. Have them stand by within an hour from the compound, by air?"

"Roger that, sir."

"Wait for my command," President Tony Sanford said and then hung up the phone without another world.

After hanging up the phone, Josh thought for a minute, and then pushed the intercom button on his phone and requested the senior agent on duty to report to him immediately.

Ten minutes later, there was a knock on his door at the same time the intercom light lit up. After he pushed the intercom button, Josh started to say, "Yes, Mary"; but did not get a chance when she said, "Josh, Agent Kyle Lasko is here."

"Enter," Josh said loud enough for Mary to hear and for Lasko to hear also, but through the intercom not the secure solid oak reinforced sound proofed door.

The door opened and in walked a tall African American, wearing a close-cropped hair cut, a mile-wide smile, blue jeans and white dress shirt, black tie and track shoes. The combination looked good on him and accented his muscular build. Walking over to Josh, he stuck out his hand to receive Josh's outstretched hand in a firm handshake.

"Thanks for coming up Kyle. How have you been? Busy, I hope," Josh asked and then indicated for Kyle to help himself to some coffee and to take a seat.

"Just returned from a little recon in Kenya and Nigeria; all is presently quiet there. Catching up on some paperwork and getting reacquainted with my wife and kids," Kyle admitted.

"Well, hate to say it, but vacation is over. I have a mission for you and your team," Josh stated and then pressed a button on his desk that immediately secured the room, locked the door, dropped a soundproof barrier in front of the only window in the room, and alerted Mary that they were not to be disturbed unless the building was on fire or under attack.

After Josh outlined the plan to Kyle, he stood and walked over to the credenza and removed a small package and handed it to Kyle.

"What's this?"

"That little device has put our organization and the President into a hell of a lot of trouble," Josh stated and then sat down again.

"Okay, was that the thing when you were kidnapped, the President was accused of murder and that island?" Kyle asked as he examined the thing that looked like a smart phone.

"Yeah, you read the report."

"Yes, but a lot was left out. Like who and how," Kyle stated.

"I know and the report you read was the sanitized one of course. The full up report is on a need to know basis. And, my friend, you have just moved into the 'Need to Know' on that op, because you are going to be waist deep in it in the next twenty-four hours." Josh paused, and then pulled out the report and handed it to Kyle. "This report is for your eyes only, not to be discussed with your team until I authorize it. I will summarize it so you can prepare."

Kyle handed the report back as Josh summarized the contents, described how the device worked, and gave him a demonstration. After twenty minutes, Kyle's eyes were wide with amazement and disbelief; but he completely understood the gravity of the situation.

"Now that you know, I need for you to get your team prepared to enter the compound in North Dakota. You will be working as members of the Department of Homeland Security, since we here at the company cannot operate legally on U.S. soil. I will be calling over there to make sure you and your team are integrated into their system. Right now, you are on standby for the op; the President is the only one that can order it a go. He will call me, and I will call you. Any questions?" Josh finished.

"Just one, boss."

"Okay."

"Where can I buy one of these? My kids would love it; hell, I love it." He handed the small projector back to Josh.

"Go, big man," Josh said with a chuckle and pressed the button that unsecured the office. Minutes after Kyle left, Josh pressed the speed dial on his secure phone to reach the President's Oval office.

"Hello sir. I have a team on standby waiting your go order. Is there anything else you want me to get started?" Josh asked and waited for Tony to reply.

"I have been talking with DHS and they are on board with your team side saddling with them, but they insist they call the shots. Their team is already in North Dakota. When can your team get there?"

"I can have them on a plane in a couple of hours, sir," Josh acknowledged.

"Make it so. Have your man report to U.R. Green, goes by the name Bob. Kind of a weak handle, but that is what he uses. Once on site, Bob is in charge. Josh, how many are on your team?" Tony asked.

"Including Kyle, there are four. We operate small effective strike teams, less chance of losing anyone."

"Good, get them in the air."

"Roger that, sir," Josh said and finally started to smile. He didn't really feel happy, just satisfied that he was able to do something to assist in getting his friends to safety.

Chapter 12 Rule Number 13

"Connie, I do believe I need a shower, care to join me?" Davin asked as he looked around the plush suite they were standing it. The room had the look and feel of a five star hotel suite, complete with wet bar, king size bed, large TV with surround sound and Blueray DVD player, a sitting room, living room, and separate bedroom. All the comforts of a nice apartment; and when they looked into the bathroom, they discovered it also had a separate shower and a hot tub big enough for four.

"Pretty nice digs, and yes, I could use a shower too," she replied as she started to undress. "Lock the door, please."

"Roger that," Davin said as he turned the lock on the door and slipped the secondary bolt over.

Minutes later, they were standing in the shower soaping each other and quietly started to discuss their situation.

"Rule number 13," Connie said as she soaped Davin's back.

"Right, trust nobody. So, what do you think of Brian?"

"Not sure, seems sincere but there are some things that just don't fit," Davin replied and then turned to soap down Connie. "You still have a beautiful sexy body for an old broad."

"I agree; how did he get to be in charge? And who killed Clark? And who is an old broad?" she teased reaching down to soap Davin below his waist, getting the response she wanted.

"Remember rule, ah, I forgot the number, but it reminds us to check for hidden cameras and microphones," Davin said looking down into her face and smiled.

"The shower and steam in here should cover any noise and visual, don't you think?" she asked as she kissed her husband passionately and pressed her soapy body into his.

"Yes, and it is getting steamier," he replied as he returned her kiss.

At the same time they were taking a shower, Sonja and Mouse were monitoring the movements of their new arrivals. They knew the two had gone into the shower, but could not hear or see what was going on; the male mercenary enjoyed watching as Connie undressed, but because of the angle of the camera could only see her back. There were no cameras or microphones in the bathroom, just in the living room; but one camera was aimed at the bathroom door, which happened to be open when Connie was getting ready for the shower. Davin had checked both rooms for cameras and microphones. He only found two in the small living room, but forgot to tell her about them until now.

"Connie, I did check the rooms; and there are two cameras and mics in the living room, none in the bedroom or bath. But keep your voice down anyway; we don't want to attract too much attention.

"Sonja, what do you think? Really on the run, or is this a very good, deep, CIA operation?" Mouse asked his partner.

"What I think doesn't matter; it is what Brian and Moose think; and from what I heard from Moose earlier, is that we need to watch these two carefully."

"Understood, my little chickadee," Mouse said with an evil laugh. Mouse had a short person complex; he only stood five foot four inches tall, small but built like an ox, always working out and building muscle upon muscle. He didn't mind being called Mouse, because he could easily whip most anyone in the compound in a fair, or unfair, fight.

His friend and companion Sonja was a workout junky too. She was able to bench press twice her own weight which wasn't really saying much because she only weighed in at about a hundred five pounds. She was quick, agile and a hell of a fighter, holding a black belt in several martial arts disciplines. Occasionally she and Mouse would spar and she could almost take him in a fair fight. If they got down and dirty, her win rate went up real fast. This meant her competitor ended up in the hospital with a few broken bones or worse. Mouse did not push her that far; he preferred keeping her at arm's length and in his bed, not looking at her from the hospital bed. Of course, when they sparred, they both held back for fear of killing one or the other.

Chapter 13 Popcorn and Movies

After a long shower, Davin and Connie dressed. But before leaving their room, they both checked the semi-automatic pistols they had picked up from the armory. They had been forced to leave their favorite weapons when they had to leave Virginia quickly. Davin, being an old Colt fan, had chosen a Colt M1911A1 with four extra magazines loaded with Hydra-shock hollow point forty-five caliber bullets. It had great stopping power in a simple to use old workhorse. He also picked up an extra box of ammo and clip on holster to carry it. Connie preferred something a bit lighter, but wanted the same stopping power; so, she picked up a Glock Model 30 forty-five caliber which held a ten round magazine. She also grabbed four additional mags and an extra box of ammo, along with a small of the back holster that made it easy to hide while wearing her casual outfits.

Brian had suggested that they keep the weapons with them at all times. When they walked out of the room, they entered the empty hallway and looked both ways, not sure which way to go, and then saw a board about fifteen feet down the hall with a building diagram posted on it.

"Maybe that will tell us where the mess hall is?" Connie suggested pointing toward the board.

"Maybe," was all that Davin said as he walked over to the board only to find a faded floor diagram with most of the letters faded away and unreadable. "Let's go this way, and see where it goes."

They started to walk to the right from their room when a voice blared over a hidden speaker, "The mess hall is the other way, Mr. Pierce."

"Ah, thank you," Davin said to the wall, and then added quietly to Connie, "Guess that answers a bunch of questions."

"Yes it does, Mr. Pierce. We have eyes and ears everywhere," the voice of Mouse stated.

"Let's go this way," Connie said and started down the hall in the direction of the mess hall. "I wonder where we can have a private conversation?"

"Only in the shower you had a few minutes ago," the voice said confirming that the shower was the only safe spot in the facility.

"Thanks for the information; by the way, what is on the menu tonight?"

"You have a choice of pork chops or meat loaf. I suggest the chops," the voice replied.

"Thanks again."

"And, yes, there is beer," the voice said without being asked.

"Good, I could use a couple right about now," Connie said only saying what Davin was thinking.

They both decided to have the pork chops accompanied by a couple of cold beers and vegetables. There were only six other people in the mess which included two behind the counter serving the food. Nobody talked much, just some quiet whispers could be heard from across the room. Davin looked up at the TV monitor on the wall and saw that the movie was going to start in the theater in twenty minutes. After completing their meal, Davin stood up and placed their trays in the window for the dishwasher and grabbed two more beers and then walked over to Connie. "Let's go to the theater baby."

Leaving the mess hall, they ran into Brian in the hall heading for the theater. "Brian, movie time?"

"Yes, follow me," Brian said and then followed up with, "Moose and most of his team will be back tomorrow. He may want to question you and Connie, be prepared for anything."

"Right," Davin commented as they entered the theater, Sue sat in the front row waiting for Brian.

"Hey, Mona we have guests. Mona Vale this is Davin and Connie Pierce; just arrived today and will be with us for a while. Did you make popcorn?"

"Yes, pleasure to meet you; hope you like the accommodations and all," Mona said, lifted the remote, turned on the TV, and increased the volume, which suddenly came from everywhere. "State of the art 8.1 sound system even has 3-D capability; but we don't turn that on too often, depending on the movie."

"You said this was an amazing facility, and now I believe it," Connie replied as she grabbed a bag of popcorn and her beer, and also sat in one of the seats in the front row. She heard and felt the sound all around her. Davin sat beside her and pulled over an Otterman to rest their feet on. "Have a seat, honey; the show is about to start. Are these reruns or new *NCIS*?"

"New, you will see Gibbs is now retired living on a boat, pops in once in a while and McGee is NCIS Director now. Tony left the series years ago to raise his new daughter that Zeva had without telling him. A couple newbies came on board, Quinn and Tory; Quinn retired. Tory is still there and is head of the team with a couple of new agents. Abby is still in the lab, but planning on retiring soon, probably her last season. Oh, Abby and Gibbs were married. Best show on television, now in its twenty-eighth season."

"Where are Bishop and Ducky?"

"Bishop has her own team in San Francisco now, and Ducky retired a couple of years ago. His young assistant, Palmer, is now head of autopsy. The show is not the same, but still number one on the charts."

Chapter 14 Below Deck

Soto walked into the lab on the *Bonaventure* and was surprised to see only half his team there. "Where is everyone?" he asked the lead scientist.

"Well, that is a good question," Greg Conway said when Soto approached him.

"Well, what is a good answer?" Soto insisted growing a little more than pissed.

"They went ashore last night. We received a call from Mason saying they were being followed and should be back to the ship by morning, as soon as they were sure they lost their tail."

"Followed by whom?" Soto yelled.

"He didn't say, but the indication I received from a text he sent later was that they were being followed by some government agents. That was nine hours ago; we have not had contact since; and when I sent a couple of the deck crew to locate them, they could not find them. We checked the police database, and they were not arrested by the local police. We have to assume they were compromised, and picked up by U.S. Customs, or worse, CIA. But why, I don't know; they are just engineers on holiday."

"That just doesn't work for me. Assemble a commando team, locate them, and get them wherever they are. Kill the ones holding them. If you can't rescue them, make sure they don't talk. Understood?" Soto ordered, not knowing who was following his men and women.

"We have a team ready to go; just waiting for you to give the go order."

"Go! NOW!" Soto screamed.

Two hours later, Conway called up to the bridge looking for Soto.

"Soto," Rocky said into the intercom.

"We have found them, and the team is heading there now. They should be on site in twenty minutes, and back here within two hours," Conway reported.

"Captain, make sure we are out of port as soon as the team is back on board," Soto said. As he started to hang up the intercom microphone, he looked out over the harbor; but before he hung up the microphone, he asked Conway, "Who has them?"

"Not any of the ones we suspected; from what I was told, it looks like a group from a Triad, oriental for sure. Possibly gangster related, maybe they were looking to kidnap our people for ransom or for human trafficking. I don't know; maybe when they return, I will ask our team to capture one of them and bring him back. We can dump him in the ocean after getting the information we need."

"Sounds like a plan, maybe bring two back and kill the rest," Soto ordered.

"I will tell the team to do that and get back as soon as possible without getting the local police involved," Conway agreed. The waiting was not something that Soto enjoyed. He was impatient and was now behind schedule. They needed to be on site in four days or his window of opportunity would close for another year. The upcoming solar eclipse that would disrupt satellite communications and much more was on May 21, 2031. He needed to be at Latitude 9.3203 degrees North by Longitude 73.8076 degrees East to get the best view of the eclipse. He was following the chart from the National Aeronautics and Space Administration. According to the chart, this would be the best place on the planet to perform his next scientific experiment. The weather forecast of the area showed that it would be clear skies and mild temperatures.

The eclipse would disrupt communications, which would open a window in the security of all the computers around the world. This gap in security would allow his team to implant software he designed into the systems around the world, giving him unlimited access to anything and everything he needed. If it worked, he could erase all the world's secrets in one quick push of a button, or take control of every bank and all the money on the planet. Every secure facility would be opened; every password would disappear; and every secret evaporate, if it worked. He wanted to cause a total melt down of life as we know it. This should work like the change in the date back in 2000 when engineers and scientists were not sure if software would work because when designed they had not planned on a major decade change from 1999 to 2000. The fear was that things would stop working altogether, banks would not be able to get to funds, elevators would stop between floors, and everything would come to a halt. That millennia scare was unfounded and nothing major happened when the systems changed. But the panic was real; and engineers around the world worked hard rewriting code and updating systems; yet it was all just a panic attack.

But his plan was not to destroy the systems but to control them, and move money to his secret numbered accounts as he needed it. He also wanted to create false intelligence that would confuse and disrupt every nation, when he wanted to.
As a side benefit to this endeavor, he had positioned a second research ship equipped with a deep submersible rescue and recovery vehicle. The second ship was preparing the deep submersible to go below the surface to retrieve the core of a lost nuclear warhead. The missile to which it was attached was fired from Iran ten years earlier and lost its guidance. Instead of detonating over its target, it turned and splashed down in the Indian Ocean. Rocky planned on retrieving the warhead and putting it to good use.

Rocky had accidently located the missile during one of his early exploration trips to the Indian Ocean for the CIA when he was a field research scientist before becoming the head of research and development. As a research scientist, he was able to travel freely to collaborate with other scientists and researchers to help him and his team develop new technology for the CIA. On one of these research ventures, he was asked to join a team of researchers in a deep sea collection mission. During one of the deep dives, he photographed and documented the missing nuclear missile. Conveniently, the operator of the deep submersible died before they reached the surface so he was not able to tell anyone. Only Rocky Soto knew of the find; and, of course, Rocky neglected to inform anyone of this find. At the time, he did not have the resources to recover the missile; but now he did.

He already had a buyer for the missile, if it was still usable, and if his team did not set it off during recovery, and of course, if he really wanted to sell it. He had several bidders for it already; ISIS was supposed to meet with him in a week to discuss the purchase. He had bidders from several African countries and other terrorist groups. He did not care what they wanted it for, although he believed that they would use it to destroy Washington DC and kill as many Americans as they could. That is what ISIS did, and he did not care. Of course, he might not sell it to them. He was considering just taking their money and killing the two buyers. But first, he needed to retrieve the warhead; it had been on the bottom of the ocean for ten years.

His personal hatred had grown over the years, since he had been fired from the CIA. He had narrowly escaped prosecution for what he did. But that was water under the bridge as they say, past history. Now he was creating a future of destruction for the world to see, the complete destruction of the United States.

It has been said that the there is a very thin line between being a genius and insanity. Rocky was walking a very thin line and which side he was on was anybody's guess.

"What is the location of those two Navy ships?" Rocky asked his radar operator when he walked onto the ship's bridge.

"They are cruising two hundred miles due east of us. One is on a heading of one seven zero, running at twelve knots. The other is converging on her at eight knots, heading three four eight degrees. Almost looks like they are going to meet about here," the operator said and pointed to a spot just west of Perth, Australia. "This is a couple hundred miles west of Perth. From there it is anybody's guess as to where they will go."

"Good, let me know immediately if they turn in our direction."

"Yes, sir," the operator said and then returned to watch his scope.

Chapter 15 Let the Chips Fall

"Brian, I heard we have guests!" boomed Moose when he entered the ranch house just before noon the next day.

"Yeah, they are taking a walk around the ranch with Sonja and Mouse right now, when do you want to meet them?" Brian replied and then flipped his grilled cheese, ham and tomato sandwich over in the frying pan. "Do you want a sandwich?"

"No, had lunch in town before driving out. But you can tell me a little about our guests before I leave to kill them," Moose stated, with a sly grin on his face.

"You are not going to kill them, Moose. They are running from the feds, wanted for murder and jail break."

"Don't tell me it is that Pierce guy and his wife? They are feds, or were feds before he popped his assistant," Moose said not expecting an answer, knowing it was Pierce. He walked over to the fridge and grabbed a beer, twisted the top off, and pitched the top into the waste can; he then took a long pull on the ice cold beer.

"Yes, it is. And we are going to hide them out for a while, just until they get some rest. Three months on the run has run them down, and they need some rest and quiet. You will not harm them in any way, Moose, or you have to answer to me; and I am not going to take any crap from you on this."

"You know if the feds find out they are here; they will come down on us hard. And we will be either dead or watching the world go by in prison," Moose said between long pulls on his beer. He finished it and grabbed a second one from the fridge.

"I know Moose, but we, no, I can't throw them out or to the wolves. They are not staying long. Just give them some time to recoup, and they will be gone," Brian said and then lifted his sandwich out of the pan and put it on a dish along with a bag of potato chips. After walking over to the table, he set it down and then reached into the refrigerator and grabbed a beer. "I will not allow you to harm them," emphasized Brian.

"Okay, but if they look like they are causing trouble, I will make sure they are gone for good. Hey, that looks good," Moose said eyeing Brian's sandwich. "That can be changed too, be careful young man. Things happen out here on the range, strange things, dangerous things," Moose added, after he recognized the subtle threat from Brian.

"The pan is over there along with the bread, ham, tomato and butter. Help yourself, this one is mine," Brian said slapping Moose's hand away from his sandwich.

"You know I could just take yours," Moose joked.

"And die trying," Brian said laughing.

"Okay, the beer will hold me for now. I am going to my room and change. Most of the guys will be back later. They will be hungry, has the chef come back yet?"

"Chef Conrad came back an hour ago and is planning a nice dinner at five thirty."

"Good, see you at dinner. Oh, are our new guests going to join us?" Moose inquired.

"Yes, they will," Brian said as he opened his chips.

"I may just kill them anyway, just for the hell of it," Moose teased and left through the back door.

"We will see about that old boy," Brian said quietly to himself as he ate his lunch. "Who's there?" he yelled when he heard the front door to the ranch house open.

"Just your local uninvited guest," Davin yelled back, "Damn that looks good."

"The fixings are over there, help yourself," Brian said pointing to the bread, cheese and tomato he had left on the counter.

"Connie, would you be the angel you usually are and fix us a couple of sandwiches. I'll fetch the beer," Davin asked sweetly.

"When you ask that way, I can't resist; you want ham on it also?"

"Yeah," he responded as he opened his beer, handed a second one to Connie, and sat down across from Brian. "Can we talk?"

"Depends on what."

"We saw a big guy come in here a bit ago. Was that Moose?" Davin asked and smiled at his wife.

"Yeah, he wants to meet you at dinner," Brian said. He then slapped Davin's hand away from his potato chips and sharply stated, "Get your own; there is a whole box over there," as he pointed at the cabinet across the room.

"Okay… Honey what kind of chips do you want, BBQ, plain, waffle?"

"Waffle, please. Your sandwich is ready," she replied as she sliced the sandwich in half and placed it on a plate. Seconds later, she walked over to the table, set her plate down, and teased Davin with his. "Where is Chilly, maybe she would like this sandwich."

"Come on baby, I'm hungry," Davin pleaded as he eyed the sandwich and his beautiful wife who loved to tease him.

"You two get a room," Brian teased back. "Oh, you have one, maybe you should use it; but there is a video camera in there, so keep it clean. Little sister and her mouse are watching most of the time."

"Good to know, thanks Brian. We found the cameras and blacked them out" Connie said.

"Now what did you want to talk about?" Brian asked picking up the last chip off his plate.

"Oh, not much, but we get the feeling that you are not telling us everything. Would you care to expand on what you have already told us?" Davin insisted and then picked up his sandwich and took a bite.

"True, I haven't told you everything; and I need permission from my brother to tell you the rest. I hope you understand. But there is a little thing called, 'Need to Know' in our world. I know you can appreciate that being who you two are. As soon as I get the go ahead, I will show you the rest; but until then you just have to trust me."

"We trust you Brian, but do not like being kept in the dark. Is there something going on here that you can, well, expand on so we are not caught with our pants down, as it were?" Connie asked and then sipped her beer.

"Yes, there is, but a question first. How do you stay so slim and drink as much beer as you do, Connie?" Brian asked.

"Exercise, a lot of exercise. And thanks for noticing; sometimes my husband forgets how much I do for him."

"Whoa, didn't mean to bring it up. But, to answer your question, I can tell you this. Moose and his band of merry men and women are planning something; and it does not include me, or Mona. I am not sure what it is, but he has been rather secretive since he returned such as holding meetings to which I am not invited, and just acting strange. He does want to kill you two; he says you will bring the Feds down on us, if they find out you are here. Well, we already know that they know you are here; and that will not happen, at least not yet. But he doesn't know that, and he doesn't know why you are really here. If he finds out, he will kill you and me as quickly as he can."

"Hell, that does make our stay a bit more interesting," Connie remarked and looked over at Davin with a smile. "Guess we may need to go down to your range and get a little practice in before we need to defend ourselves. What do you think, Davin?"

"Not a bad idea. Is the range open for use today?" Davin asked.

"Yeah, here is the key to the armory. Pick up some more ammo and go punch holes in some targets; there is a stack beside the door. Have a good time, but watch your backs. And you may want to get a backup pistol while in the armory," Brian suggested.

"Not a bad idea, Brian. Thanks for the sandwich," Davin said as he stood and walked over to the fridge. He reached in and grabbed a couple of sodas instead of beer. "Beer and guns don't mix too well, so we will have to settle for soda, honey."

"Make mine an orange juice, soda doesn't agree with me," Connie said. She stood up, and took the plates to the dishwasher where she rinsed them and then slipped them into the washer.

"If you need us, we will be on the range, Brian," Connie said; and they stepped out the back door and headed for the elevator in the barn to go down to the range.

Chapter 16 Things That Go Bump in the Dark

The sun did not set until late during the summer months in the mid-west. This was an advantage if you preferred to take a walk after dinner and wanted it to be sunny but cool when you did. But this was not summer, it was the beginning of fall and the days were getting shorter.

Dinner was at five-thirty. Davin and Connie sat alone at one of the tables near the corner; and Davin sat with his back to the wall. An old habit he always did, especially in a new setting. He was positioning himself so he could see the entire room; and it usually provided that nobody could shoot him in the back.

Shortly after Davin and Connie got their food and sat at a table in the corner of the mess hall, Brian and Moose walked in and headed toward them.

"Davin, Connie, I would like you to meet George Monahan; around here, he is known as Moose. Moose, this is Davin and Connie Pierce." Brian introduced each of them. Moose reached over and shook Davin's outstretched hand, adding a little more pressure than needed in a friendly greeting.

"Pleasure to meet you, may we join you?" Moose asked in a most civil tone.

"Sure, get your food and come on over," Davin said.

"Be right back," Brian said and both of them turned and headed for the cafeteria style counter to get their dinner. They returned a few minutes later with full trays of food and drink.

Halfway through dinner, the intercom blared, "Attention in the compound, will Brian and or Moose contact the office immediately."

"Damn, what the hell is it now?" Brian said, "Always interrupting my dinner."

"I will take care of it, Brian," Moose said, standing. "If it requires your assistance, I will let you know." He walked over to the wall phone and picked up the handset and punched three numbers to connect to the office. "This is Moose. What's the problem?" he said. After listening for a moment, he hung up the phone, walked back to the table, leaned over, and whispered in Brian's ear.

"Shit, let's go," Brian said and stood, "Excuse us, emergency upstairs."

Brian and Moose walked quickly to the exit; and then when they were in the hall, they started to run as fast as they could to the elevator.

Upon reaching the office, they were informed that there were trespassers on the north side of the ranch. The ranch was over nine hundred acres and the intruders were spotted on the inside of the fence north of the ranch house, about three miles away.

"What do you want to do?" the security guard asked when they saw the view on the camera.

"Six armed intruders. Are they hunters? They look like hunters. They are not carrying assault rifles; those are bolt action hunting rifles," Brian said as he looked closely at the monitor. "Send out a couple of our guys to let them know they are on private land and suggest that they go back the way they came. If they don't want to go that way, then put them in the truck and drive them to the main road."

"I will go," Moose suggested.

"No, I need you here in case they are not what they seem to be."

"I will put together my backup team and wait in the barn. I will send Mouse and Sonja up there; it may be dark by the time they get there. But they can handle it. They will have automatic weapons in case there is a problem; and we will maintain constant open mic with them."

"Good idea. Make it so, Moose."

"Roger that, boss."

"Alfred, monitor them and let me know if there is a problem. I will be in the mess hall," Brian said and walked out of the office.

The sun had set by the time Sonja and Mouse arrived at the north fence and found the six hunters. They drove right up to the campsite, and stopped about twenty feet from the hunters who were sitting on the ground around a quickly made campfire.

"Hello gentlemen," Sonja yelled as she stepped out of the truck, leaving the headlights on, shining on the six.

"Hello. What can we do for you?" one of the men yelled back.

"Do you know you are on private property?" Sonja asked.

"No, didn't see a sign or fence." he replied, standing up with his rifle cradled in his arm and hand near the trigger but not on it.

"That's strange, we have a fence all the way around the property with signs, didn't you see them?" She stated as Mouse slid out of the passenger seat, standing behind the door with his Mac-10 out of sight.

"No, we saw no fence. We just want to camp here tonight and then we will leave first thing in the morning," the man stated.

"We can't allow that, sir. This is private property and you have to leave, now." The rest of the men stood with their rifles in their hands and spread out to make it more difficult to shoot all of them easily. It was obvious they were military trained and were preparing for trouble. Two of them slipped just to the edge of the headlight beams.

"It would be foolish for us to attempt to move during the night; not knowing the lay of the land, it would be suicidal."

"It would also be suicidal for you to stay here any longer," Sonja stated in a very stern voice.

"Look, lady, let us stay for the night; and we will move back north first thing in the morning."

"No, you will lay your weapons down and get into the back of the truck. We will drive you to the main road and you can get back to town that way," Sonja insisted.

"No, we are staying right here," the man replied, raised his rifle, and shot out one of the headlights.

"Bad move mister," Mouse yelled and raised his Mac 10 and fired a short burst at the six hunters. Sonja grabbed for her Mac 10, but did not reach it when a bullet ripped into her shoulder throwing her to the ground. The exchange of fire ended with four well placed bullets from the team's snipers. Sonja and Mouse were on the ground dead. None of the six hunters were injured or even came close to being hit.

"Okay, time to go," the leader of the six said quietly as he looked over at Sonja and Mouse. "Get their weapons and disable the truck.

"Boss, I do believe I already disabled the truck," one of the snipers said when she walked into the campfire light and pointed to the steam coming from under the hood of the truck. She strolled over to the body of Mouse, picked up his Mac 10, and removed a Berretta 9 mm from a holster he was wearing. "Snickers hit the battery, and I put a bullet in the radiator and engine block; this truck will not go very far."

"Hawkeye, get their weapons and made sure you get her pistol too. We may need them," the boss ordered Beth, aka Hawkeye, as he kicked dirt on the fire. He switched off the holographic transmitter and the hunters disappeared. The hunting rifles instantly changed into what they were originally, M4 assault rifles. Within minutes, the rest of the team walked into the campsite making the full complement of ten including two snipers with spotters, a communications specialist, ordinance expert, medical and backups for each. They were a perfect Special Ops or Seal team, but they actually were elite members of a Special Weapons and

Tactics (SWAT) team formed by the Department of Homeland Security (DHS).

Beth, call sign Hawkeye, was tall, five foot nine inches with fire red hair and green eyes; she had the body of a model and was deadly with or without a weapon, scoring fourth in the top ten of all the Army snipers presently serving their country. She was also the communications officer within her team, holding a master's degree in computer and electronic engineering.

Michelle, aka Snickers, her near twin, stood five foot six; she also had the body of a model yet was shorter with blonde hair, and blue eyes. She was an ex-surfer from California who had joined the Navy right out of college and easily passed the exam to become a sniper. She held a master's degree in criminology from Berkley and two gold medals for marksmanship. She also placed third in the top ten of all snipers past and present. Unlike her partner Beth, she preferred to carry the lighter Remington M24 that was similar to the Remington 700 bolt action but used the .300 Winchester Magnum round.

Whereas Beth preferred the heavier Barrett M-82A1 (SM107) chambered for the 50 caliber round, powerful, but heavy, and considered more of a long range sniper rifle, especially for its stopping power. It had a maximum effective range of one thousand five hundred meters for material targets and one thousand meters for personnel. However, each weapon had great performance, and either enabled the sniper to reach out and touch their targets without hesitation.

The Navy did not let women serve on Seal Teams and that policy prevented Michelle from becoming a Seal. Even though these two females had proven to the world that they were just as tough and did not shy from a fight, they were not satisfied with the decision to prevent Michelle from becoming a Seal. Beth, on the other hand, had more opportunities because the Army did allow females to become Rangers and Special Forces. But that was not enough for her; she wanted Special Ops and when turned down, they both left the service when their enlistment was up and joined the Department of Homeland Security as snipers. Better pay, better hours and they were at the top of their game. They had proven once again that women could be just as tough as men and still look like Victoria Secret models. Both were trained snipers and damn good at taking out targets, with more than twenty confirmed kills between them.

The Department of Homeland Security had formed a SWAT team and when they offered Beth and Michelle a better opportunity than the Army or Navy could, they jumped at it. Their new boss was ex-SEAL Commander Ulysses Robert Green; he was six-foot-tall, had hazel eyes and sandy hair. He was muscular and extremely competent.

The SWAT team left the carnage behind, and walked slowly south toward the ranch house. They had lost the element of surprise, but still had a few tricks up their sleeves. The mission they had been given was to remove Brian, his partner, and the Pierce couple from the compound. This team had never failed in a mission, and they were not about to fail now. Things had changed in the few days since they had gone undercover in the compound and the Department of Homeland Security had deemed it necessary to extract ahead of schedule.

An hour after the shootout, Moose and his team showed up to find Sonja and Mouse dead, the truck damaged beyond repair, and no sign of the intruders.

"Spread out and find those sons a bitches!" he ordered. "Damn, whoever they are, they are packing some heavy artillery, looks like a fifty took out the truck and whatever hit Mouse was at least a magnum," he said as he examined the damage.

Chapter 17 What You Don't See Can Hurt You

Davin and Connie have been at the compound for two days; and in that time, two of the mercenaries had been killed and six were missing. Davin and Connie had been confined to the first floor of the facility and were under the watchful eye of two guards.

"Wonder who is causing the ruckus up there?" Connie asked as they lay in bed.

"Have no idea, but if I were a betting man, which I am, I would say that Josh somehow found out something that we don't know and sent in the cavalry. Or at least a Seal Team, Special Ops or one of those highly trained SWAT type teams; they do have military training, and when they want to talk to us they will," Davin said as he stared at the ceiling.

"You think he knows," Connie questioned.

"Yeah, he knows."

"What are we going to do?" Connie asked.

"Well, it seems that whoever they are, they can't be seen or caught. I think we just ride it out and see what happens. Moose won't let us go; Brian needs our help; and whoever they are is causing some problems for Moose," Davin concluded and then walked into the bathroom. He stopped suddenly when he came face to face with a tall sandy haired man dressed in full combat gear holding his finger to his lips to silence Davin.

Davin walked over to the shower, turned the water on high, and waited before quietly saying, "How the hell did you get in here? And who are you?"

"One question at a time, Mr. Pierce; I am just a simple soldier. First, we are here to get you, Mrs. Pierce, Brian and his partner out. I am Ulysses Green, Department of Homeland Security; you can call me Bob," Green whispered.

"DHS, wow, when did they get into the SWAT business? Kind of a lame handle, isn't it?" Davin questioned as he studied the intruder.

"My middle name is Robert, and several years ago, but that doesn't matter right now. We have been ordered to get you out of here," Bob stated seriously.

"We just arrived; why pull us out now? And by whose orders?" Davin protested.

"All I know is that we are to pull all of you out now. My orders come from DHS. They have intel showing Rocky Soto is in the Indian Ocean on a ship, doing what we don't know. We have two destroyers heading toward them to take him down. Mr. Randal has four of his men assigned with me, you may know Kyle Lasko." "Yes, I know Kyle, is he with you?" Davin said and then continued, "Soto, in the Indian Ocean? Okay, so what is the plan?" Davin asked quietly. "And why take us out now?"
"Not sure, not important at the moment. Now get your wife in here and get ready to leave. My team is well hidden, but it is only a matter of time before we are found," Green stated and then pointed toward the door indicating that he wanted Connie to come in.

Two minutes later, Connie was standing in front of the mirror looking at Ulysses Green, who was standing behind the door behind her.

"How did you get in here?" she asked looking confused as she turned around to look him in the face. Green pointed straight up at the air conditioner intake vent.

"Oh," she replied, looking up at the ceiling.

"And that is how we are leaving. You two are going to follow me. There are two guards outside your door, we could take them out, but that would just send up the alarm and we want to exit quietly, as quietly as possible."

"Okay, let's go," Davin said and then stopped and asked, "What about Brian?"

"Lasko is getting them right now; they will meet us at a prearranged location in fifteen minutes," Green stated and then reached up and opened the vent.

"Should we get our weapons?" Connie asked.

"No, they probably don't work anyway or the bullets are fake; one or the other."

"I checked them out completely, they are fully functional," Davin stated feeling a bit insulted.

"We have weapons for you. Now can we go?" Green said and then pulled himself up through the vent and then looked back down and extended his arm down to help Connie up. They were lucky to still be completely dressed when Green showed up. Davin reached over, turned off the water in the shower, and then was helped up into the vent. He pulled the vent closed behind him and followed Green in between the floors of the compound.

The area between floors was not tall, only a little more than a crawl space; but when the facility was built, it was designed to make it much easier to modify and add new equipment with the associated cabling. Between each floor was a four-foot-high crawl space that allowed for new cabling and ducting to be run easily from one section to another. Only a few people knew about this, Brian being one, and of course the long dead designers. If anyone looked at the blue prints, they would also know about the crawl space; but the prints were classified, and held in only two places, Brian's office and the Department of Defense archives.

Prior to leaving on this mission, Kyle Lasko visited the DoD archives and found the blue prints, discovered the crawl space that allowed the team to penetrate the facility, and used it to hide from Moose and his militia.

Chapter 18 Change of Plans

May 21, 2031 started out as what anyone would expect for a summer day in the Indian Ocean. Rocky Soto and his team were working hard getting their equipment ready for what he hoped to be the end of all the security on the Internet. When the eclipse occurred later today, they would activate their equipment by aiming it at the sun, which in theory would intensify the signal and attach itself to all the Wi-Fi towers and satellites around the world. Once the virus hit, within minutes, it should destroy all firewalls, virus scanners, passwords and anything that remotely resembled a security program. Of course, it would supposedly only work if all computers, servers and associated systems were turned on.

"Six hours until total eclipse, Rocky," Greg announced and then said, "We are ready and both programs are ready, the take down and the removal."

"Good, I will be in my cabin. I need to contact Horatio," Rocky said as he started for the door. "I will be back in time to witness the take down."

"Are you sure our banks can handle the transfer of that much cash?" Greg asked.

"Sixteen banks with secure accounts that are just begging to be filled. Make it so, Gregory; make it so! We will all be very rich men when done," Soto said and then walked out of the lab and headed toward his cabin just as the ships intercom barked, "Mr. Soto, would you come to the bridge as soon as you can," the voice said.

"Crap, what does the Captain need now?" Soto said and turned toward the ladder to the bridge. Three minutes later, Soto entered the bridge. "What is it, Captain?"

"We have trouble heading our way. The two Navy ships are heading directly toward us, should arrive in about two hours; they are just over the horizon. They are steaming at about thirty knots.

We were able to get a satellite shot of them, warships, or destroyers most likely, and they are coming to us."

"How did you miss them turning our way; they were over two hundred miles away when I checked earlier?" Soto yelled.

"I don't know, sir; we have been watching them, and then suddenly they just disappeared from where they were and showed up heading for us at flank speed. Almost like they pulled a Star Trek on us and turned on their cloaking device," the operator stated, "I have been watching them the whole time; and they were still close to Perth, Australia until a few minutes ago."

"They must have some kind of technology to mask their actual location, maybe send false signals, I don't know. Damn, if I am here, this whole thing goes to hell. It is at least four hours before we can make it happen. Get the chopper ready, I will leave for now; the test can go on without me," Soto ordered and then headed off the bridge and to his cabin. Along the way, he stopped for a minute at the lab and ordered, "Greg, you are now a weather ship here to measure the intensity of the eclipse and its effect on communications."

"Of course, sir, we are prepared for that; now go, if you are caught here all is lost," Gregory stated and then turned back to his team and issued orders to change their screens to a special program he had designed just in case this happened.

"Wait, only do the take down and transfer of cash, do not do the removal of anything. I have a better idea as to what to do with the secrets of the world," Soto said before leaving the lab.

Twenty minutes later, he was leaving the helo pad in a modified Bell Jet Ranger. It would take a couple of hours to get to India where he had contracted a Gulfstream VII for immediate departure with a destination of San Francisco. But, upon entering the helicopter, he ordered his pilot to turn west and go to his other ship; he needed to check on progress before leaving for San Francisco.

Two hours and fifteen minutes after Soto left the *Bonaventure*, the guided missile destroyer *USS O'Kane* (DDG 77) and the *USS Nicholson* (DD982) were sitting about fifty yards off of the ship. The *O'Kane* dispatched two of her whalers with armed marines to board the *Bonaventure*.

"*Bonaventure*, this is the Captain of the *USS Nicholson*, please prepare to be boarded," the Captain said over the radio to the radio operator of the *Bonaventure*.

"Yes, sir, we are lowering the boarding ladder on the port side," the operator replied per the instructions given him by his captain.

Minutes later, the captain of the *Bonaventure* was standing on the main deck waiting for the boarding party to come up the stairs.

"Good afternoon, sir. What is the meaning of this? We are a research vessel here to view and measure the eclipse which will happen in just under two hours."

"Sir, we have reports that a fugitive is onboard your vessel and need to conduct a search," the commander of the boarding party stated. "May we conduct our search?"

"By all means, sir, just be aware that our research cannot be stopped. This event will not happen again for many years. You may go anywhere you wish and ask your questions. If you need a guide, I will provide your men with whatever you need," the captain said quietly.

"Thank you sir," the commander said, then turned and ordered his men to disperse and start their search. "This should not take long Captain. If you have nothing to hide, we should be gone within the hour, two at the most; and you can continue with your research. May I accompany you to the bridge?"

"I have a fresh pot of coffee in the galley if you prefer."

"That sounds great. Lead on, sir," the commander agreed and then followed the Captain to the galley while his men conducted their search.

Chapter 19 Escape from Seventy Below

Green, Connie and Davin crawled through the space between the floors for about fifteen minutes before Green stopped and held up his hand for them to stop and be quiet. He continued on for a few feet and then stopped and peered down through a ceiling vent. The ducting had been moved to allow access to the vent and the room below.

After a few seconds of listening and looking, he signaled for Connie and Davin to move toward him, indicating for them to stay quiet. Green pointed to his eyes and then to Davin and Connie and indicated for them to look down through the vent. What they saw was not what they had expected to see. Lying on a sofa directly below them was a beautiful German Shepherd, sound asleep. Beside the shepherd, stood a tall bald soldier dressed in combat fatigues and holding an M4A1 Assault rifle.

"Who's the big guy with the gun?" Connie asked quietly looking very impressed with what she was seeing.

"That's Jefferson and you have probably already met Chilly. Now let's go," Green said and then opened the vent. Chilly woke and looked up also without a growl, but did show her teeth. After seeing whom it was, she laid her head back down, and closed her eyes. Green dropped down beside Jefferson, reached up to help Connie down, and then watched as Davin dropped quietly to the floor.

"Where are we?" Davin asked quietly.

"We are close to the elevators and the stairwell to the surface," Green said and then looked down the hallway outside the door. "Still clear, we sit tight here for a bit and then with luck we sneak to that stairwell and up into the darkness. We will take the stairs, will take a little longer going up, but I can't risk being trapped in the elevator. Up there, we will join up with the rest of my team, Brian Forest, and his other partner. From there, we will leave the compound. We have helicopters on standby to fly us away from here. We have to be gone before sunrise," Bob said and looked down at Chilly.

"Why, is something going to happen at dawn?" Connie inquired.

"All hell is going to break loose; and we don't want to be anywhere near here," Green said; and then said, "Forgive me, this is Mark Jefferson; this is Davin and Connie."

"Figured that, boss."

"And that on the sofa is Chilly, best guard dog in the west according to the classified report I read on Forest and his partners," Green said pointing toward the sleeping German Shepherd.

"We met her earlier. Why is she here with you? Thought she was Brian's partner," Davin asked.

"She is, Brian sent her to check on a problem in the barn when she discovered us; luckily I knew the password and so did she, and she has been with us for the past hour," Jefferson said, smiling. "We assume she will hang with us until Brian joins in and then go with him."

Upstairs, the remainder of Green's team was playing hide and seek with several militia members. It was a game and the good guys were winning, for now. Moose's group of mercenaries only hoped to be as good as Green's DHS team, but sometimes the numbers don't lie. And Moose had the numbers; it was thirty-eight mercenaries to ten DHS and one very well-trained dog. Even with the help of Davin, Connie, Brian and Mona, they were outnumbered. But history has taught us that even a small force could win in the numbers game, if they played their cards right. DHS had already reduced the numbers against them by six. Those six were nicely wrapped up in a secured room at the lowest level of the facility. They would be found if and when Moose took the time to look for them; in the meantime, Green's group would add to the captured mercenaries, one or two at a time.

Lieutenant Bell was doing his best to keep his team intact and the mercenaries chasing ghosts. The weather was cooperating with the wind kicking up to about twenty-five miles per hour; the sun had set and the moon was casting shadows which helped in their ability to run a successful hide and seek scenario.

"Snickers and Hawkeye, are you under cover?" Bell asked quietly over the unit's secure communications that every member wore while in a combat situation.

"Roger, LT. I have two; no make that four B.G.s at your two o'clock moving from your left to right. They look like they are on a mission, oh, yeah, to find you. I suggest staying put for a moment," Snickers commented quietly.

"Bob, what's your status?"

"Stuck for the moment; we should be moving out of here in twenty or less," Green said quietly and peered down the hall again. "LT, can you kill the generators, and put us in the dark?"

"Give me ten, and dark it will be," Bell said. He turned to two of his men, pointed to them, and signaled for them to move out. They had heard the order from Green, and knew where the generators were; they immediately moved out to complete the mission.

The generators were located in a building that looked very much like a stable that could hold at least thirty horses but had only six horses. There were six generators on the property, two in the stables, two back-up generators in the barn, and two deep below the surface which were vented to the surface. None of them were in use presently because power was being supplied by the local electric company. If the local company failed to supply power for more than four minutes, two of the generators would automatically start and switch over to operate the facility. Because of the size and power consumption required by the facility, it required that two generators would start and supply power, but this depended on the load being drawn. Since the facility was not fully functional, only one generator would start; but which one, the team did not know.

So, the plan was to disable all of them and then kill the local power coming in, which would put the entire facility in the dark.

The two DHS members slowly moved from their protected position heading toward the stable to disable those generators, but did not get very far.

The first bullet slammed into the wall less than an inch from the lead man's head. Immediately both men dropped to the ground, turned and fired short bursts in the direction of the shooter. They only staying down for a second to site in where the shooter was firing from before getting up to run for better cover. The second and subsequent bullets rained down on the two DHS members, striking the second member in the shoulder, spinning him around and causing him to land on his back with his weapon pointing in the wrong direction. Hurt and bleeding, he rolled over and returned fire with his M4A1 rifle. With bullets striking all around them, they slowly, but as quickly as possible, low crawled backwards behind a small pickup truck.

"Snickers, do you see the shooters?"

"Negative, I can't see them, but maybe I can rattle their cage, standby. The shot came from a small concrete bunker," Snickers said. She took aim on the spot where she could see the bunker from which the shooters were firing. She chambered a smart bullet with an explosive head into her Remington M24 and sited in on the bunker. The bullet was designed to penetrate up to six inches of concrete, but this old facility probably had eight to twelve inch walls. It was supposed to be nuclear hardened, and she was about to find out how thick the walls were.

"Hawkeye, any luck on the shooter?" Bell asked.

"No, I am on the wrong angle to the target."

Slowly Snickers squeezed the trigger and felt the recoil of her magnum. She watched as the bullet travelled the approximately six hundred yards before striking the back of the bunker and exploding. The explosion was not massive, but the destruction was larger than she expected. The shooting from the bunker stopped immediately after the exploding bullet hit, giving her team mates time to get to a better cover position. Seconds later, the shooting started again from the bunker.

"What the hell was that?" one of the mercenaries yelled at his buddy; both their ears were ringing and their eyes watering, but neither one suffered anything more than a headache.

"How do I know? It sounded like someone set off a bomb on our back door. Keep shooting, we need to keep them down until Carl and Sam get behind them," the other mercenary yelled back as he dropped his empty magazine and slipped in a fresh one.

"That rattled their cage a bit; let's up the ante a bit," Bell ordered, and he and one of his men started toward his pinned down men. They didn't get three feet before his partner was hit in the chest by another mercenary. The firefight had started. Bell and his man returned fire in the direction of the sniper. "Shooter on top of the barn," Bell pointed out to Snickers and Hawkeye.

"Roger, LT," Snickers acknowledged and raised her aim to see the silhouette of a shooter lying on the peak of the barn roof firing down at Bell and his teammate. "Smile, ass hole," she said just as she pulled the trigger of her M24. "Oops!" she mumbled when she saw that the bullet she had fired was another smart explosive one. When it struck the sniper, it literally blew the sniper in half. She reloaded another explosive round and aimed at the bunker; the sun was down, so it was difficult to see, so she switched on her infrared and saw that there were two shooters in the bunker. Scanning the bunker, she saw a construction seam running vertically, or was it the seam to a door. Before firing, she reprogrammed the bullet to penetrate before exploding. With luck, the bullet would penetrate six to ten inches before exploding, causing death and destruction to anyone inside. She would soon find out. She squeezed the trigger, and sent her next explosive bullet into the seam.

"Bell, we can't wait, we are coming out," Green said and with his small entourage they exited the facility through the barn stairwell and exited right into a firefight.

"Hurry!" Bell replied as he continued to fire toward a new source of fire. "Looks like they are bringing in everyone for target practice and we are targets."

"Two targets down," Hawkeye commented over the comm link.

"Take out as many as you see, ladies," Green ordered quickly.

"Roger that, boss man," Hawkeye reported back.

"Your wish is our command, boss man," Snickers replied. Both Hawkeye and Snickers laid down some heavy fire taking out any of the militia they could either see or could see where they were hiding. Within seconds, both were taking return fire from several militias that they had not taken out. They never let up and shot eight more militias; the shots from the militia were falling short of their intended targets, so both were not worried about being hit. Their weapons could reach out and touch the enemy at any time. And the time was now; six more militia hit the dirt never to rise again.

"Good shooting, ladies," Green said calmly into his headset. "We may just make it out of here, yet." He paused for a second, looked up over the top of the ranch house, and saw a helicopter approaching. It wasn't one of his. "What the hell!" he exclaimed.

"Boss, should we take it out?" Hawkeye asked.

"No, wait; let's see who is dropping in," Green ordered and then switched channels to call in his own helicopters, four total, two Apache gunships and two Super Blackhawks equally equipped with missiles and Gatling guns. The Blackhawks would pick up the wounded and rest of the team, while the Apaches would lay down very heavy cover fire.

The bad guys had lost most of their team, leaving only six standing and returning fire. Among those was Moose; he was armed with a Chinese made AK-47.

"Hell, who are these guys?" he asked nobody in particular; but was concerned that most of his force had been killed or wounded.

Chapter 20 Dropping In

Approaching from the south was a new model Bell Jet Ranger 206 flying low over the ranch. It was a civilian model that was unarmed, but was capable of carrying an assortment of weapons if it was the military model. The pilot came in low with his lights on and looking for a spot to land. Banking abruptly to the left when the pilot saw they flash of gunfire, he decided to move to a safe distance before landing.

"What the hell is going on down there?" Soto asked from the back of the helicopter.

"Looks like a firefight between your guys and what looks like a Special Forces group. Can't tell who is winning, so we will land on the other side of the ranch house," the pilot commented as he turned the helicopter out of the firefight.

The militia was caught off guard and stopped firing, but not for long. However, it was just long enough for Bob and his team to regroup in a secure location.

Upon seeing the Bell land on the other side of the ranch house, Moose signaled to two of his men to find out who was onboard that helo, and to radio him as soon as they knew. Three rounds slammed into the side of the wall that Moose was kneeling behind. "Who the hell are those guys?" he asked himself, again.

"Bandleader Six, Bandleader One, do you copy?" Green said into his microphone and received nothing but static. He repeated the call twice more before getting a reply.
"Bandleader One this is Six, sorry, below the ridge and could barely hear you. Got you five by five, now; Go!" the response came over the radio indicating that he was now receiving the signal loud and clear.

"Ready to extract, HOT LZ, repeat HOT LZ. Come in HOTTER!"

"Roger, Boss, Calvary on the way, keep your heads down."

"Chilly, go find Brian and Mona; get them up here," Green ordered Chilly, and she took off running down the stairs from inside the barn.

On the opposite side of the ranch house, the Bell Jet Ranger touched down gently and immediately Soto flung open the door only to be stopped by two armed, very pissed off militia men. "Who the Hell are you?" one yelled over the noise of the rotor blades, as they looked at an old, heavy set gentleman in a gray suit and his silver haired assistant.

"Who the hell am I? Who the hell are you? And what the hell is going on over there?" Soto yelled back as he walked quickly over to the two men.

"We were sent over here by Moose to find out who you were; now are you going to tell me, or do I have to shoot you first?"

"I am the guy who is paying for all this. Now put down your weapons and get me to Richard Clark!" Soto demanded; and then followed with a short caveat, "Or she will shoot you, and she never misses." He pointed toward his assistant Tara, dressed as an elderly, silver haired woman holding an M-4 automatic rifle that she pointed directly at both men.

"Clark is dead; Brian Forest is now in charge, and Moose, or rather George Monahan, is his second. We don't know where Forest is, but I can take you to Moose if you have her lower that," he said pointing his finger at Tara.

"Sounds like World War Three over there," Soto said as the intensity of the shooting increased.

Green's helos laid down heavy cover fire, while Davin, Connie, Green and the rest of his team climbed on board. The four wounded were loaded in with Davin and Connie. The helos were just about to lift off, when Chilly came running toward the first helo with something in her mouth.

Green jumped down, met her halfway, and took the note. After quickly reading it, he patted Chilly on the head, dove back into the chopper, and yelled, "GO!"

Chilly jumped in the chopper just as it started to lift and snuggled up to Connie for the ride.

The two Apaches laid down enough cover fire to allow everyone to board and leave the area. Hawkeye, Snickers and their two spotters were to be picked up about two miles up range at a prearranged location.

"What did Chilly give you, Green?" Connie asked as they flew out of range of the militia.

"The note said to pick Brian and Mona up at the end of runway three six. Where the hell is runway three six?" Green replied.

"North end of the lake, there is a runway just under the surface," Connie replied. "Davin are you okay?"

Not getting a response from Davin, she leaned down and put her hand on his shoulder. She immediately became worried and then noticed blood on the back of his neck.

"Davin, Davin!" she yelled and shook him. "Davin's been hit."

Green reached over and checked for a pulse and did not find one. He immediately signaled to the pilot to go as fast as he could to land at runway three six to pick up Brian and Mona. As he looked over at Connie, he shook his head and said, "He's gone. Sorry." *'Damn, we need to take this place down and move in,'* Green stated to himself.

Without saying a word or breaking into a crying fit, Connie pushed the door gunner aside and took control of the 50 caliber machine gun and started to fire back into the compound. Her bullets slammed into everything destroying parts of the barn and ranch house. No one, out in the open, stood a chance of survival. She only hoped that whoever fired that last shot was one of her targets. Then she spotted Moose, standing beside the ranch house north wall. He was smiling when they made eye contact, but immediately his smile turned into a scared look. He knew his days were numbered, and that his killing of Davin Pierce just unleased a woman bent on revenge who would not stop until he was dead. Moose raised his rifle, took aim on Connie, and slowly pulled the trigger, as 50 caliber rounds slammed all around him. His AK-47 was no match for the 50 and he knew it; but if he were lucky, he could kill her and end this right now. The only sound he heard was the unmistakable click of an empty rifle.

"Damn!" Moose exclaimed to no one as he reached for another magazine and found none available; he was completely out of bullets.

"Give me more ammo and turn this damn chopper around; I want to kill that son of a bitch," Connie yelled over the noise of the chopper as her weapon ran out of bullets. The only audible sounds were her heavy breathing and the sound of the rotor blades spinning. They were moving out of range of her weapon fast. "Now, why was it so important to blow our cover, and get Davin killed, WHY?" she yelled at Green.

"We need to go. Sit down. I will explain once we pick up Brian and Mona," Bob Green answered and then to himself, 'Damn, this has turned into a shitty day.'

"Moose will soon learn how much of a bitch I can be, take me back there NOW!" Connie ordered.

"No, not now, you will get your chance. Right now, is not the time; we need to get back," Green ordered grabbing hold of her as she cried.

Just outside the ranch house, Moose sat smiling; he was shaking his head in disbelief. "I just killed Davin Pierce. Hell is going to rain down on us now. We need to get the hell out of here and fast," he said to the soldier sitting beside him.

"That was a lucky shot, boss. I saw the ricochet off that soldier's helmet."

"I don't know about lucky; I wanted that leader to go down, and he moved just as I pulled the trigger. The bullet skimmed off his helmet into Pierce's head. Damn, a shit storm is coming; we need to move and fast."

"Roger that, boss. I will gather the boys."

"We need to find Brian," Moose commented as he stood and looked over at the bodies of his men scattered around the ranch. "Get me a count of how many we lost and who, and find Forest!"

"Will do, sir."

"Don't call me, sir, damn it," Moose yelled, "Now go."

Chapter 21 Who's In Charge Now

Twenty minutes after landing, Soto was standing in front of a large man that was bleeding slightly from a scratch on his forehead.

"You should have that attended to, Mr. Monahan," Soto commented as he closely looked at the man.

"It's nothing, what can I do for you?" Moose asked and then added, "We are looking for Brian Forest, but have not been able to locate him; he may have been taken by that force that just flew out of here. We are also looking for three other missing personnel who may or may not be alive or even on the compound anymore."

"Other than Mr. Forest, I hope the missing personnel are of nobody of consequence."

"Nobody will miss any of them, but we would like to account for everyone. That group came in for something, maybe just to kidnap Forest; maybe the others were just in the way, and they took them too. We just don't know yet," Moose commented and then looked over at his lieutenant and nodded, giving him the right to depart and to account for everyone. "I know we have never met, sir, so I have no idea what to call you other than sir."

"Did not Mr. Clark tell you about me?" Soto asked.

"No, sir, he only said we had a benefactor and nothing more and for me not to ask any questions. And being a good officer, I did not ask, I assumed, but that only gets you into more trouble."

"Good, good. Mr. Monahan, I am Soto, Horatio Soto. May we go inside and get a cup of tea or Saki if you have some," Soto said and looked around to see if he could find an entrance and could not.

"This way Mr. Soto, follow me; we have a full bar downstairs and believe we can come up with some Saki or most anything else you prefer."

"Oh, this is my assistant Tara Wong. She likes tea."

"No problem Mr. Soto and Miss Wong."

Minutes later with drinks and sitting in a quiet conference room just down the hall from the cafeteria, they sat and sipped their drinks quietly.

"What brings you to our humble compound, Mr. Soto?" Moose asked between sips of his beer.

"It is simple, Mr. Monahan. When I made my arrangements with Clark, I instructed him that I would send money to build your team with the condition that he would do a few jobs for me when I needed them done. The time has come for him, now you, to fulfill my wishes."

"I know nothing about your arrangement with Clark, so I am not sure I can comply with your wish," Moose stated declining to continue with the arrangement.

"Oh, but you have to. The money has been paid as promised and it is now time, as you may say, to pay the piper."

"But we have not seen any money for months; well, for at least four months," Moose interjected thinking that maybe Forest had gotten it and just not passed it down. But no, Forest would not do that, or would he?

"A deal is a deal; maybe your head man did not tell you about the money arriving and kept it for himself. I have a job for you, and you will do it when I say so. Or, for sure, I will cut off any more money; and well, let's just say your days of breathing fresh North Dakota air will be shortened, considerably, along with the balance of your men. Do I make myself clear, Mr. Monahan?" Soto stated without smiling.

"Are you threatening me, Soto? The last man that did that is lying up on the side of the hill in a six-foot hole. Would you care to..." Moose said almost yelling until he felt the cold point of a pistol pressed to the side of his head. "I could take that from you little lady before..." he started to say, when he heard a click of the hammer being pulled back.

"I would not try that Mr. Monahan; she is faster than the bullet in the art of killing. Trust me, I have seen her at work; and besides being extremely beautiful, she is extremely dangerous."

"Okay, say we do the job, then what?" Moose agreed quietly. "Please ask her to remove the gun from my ear, sir."

A second later, Tara walked around in front of Moose holding a small flute in her right hand. Moose looked at that and could not believe he had mistaken a small metal flute for a weapon until he saw a long, very sharp, stiletto blade in her left hand.

"Cutting of the throat or piercing the heart is much quieter than a gunshot, Mr. Monahan; and if done properly, would yield very little blood. Now are you ready to comply with my wishes, Mr. Monahan?" Soto asked again.

"What about Brian Forest, do we just cut him out?"

"Yes, for now, or at least until we know what has become of him and the other personnel you are missing."

"What is this job you want us to do?"

"I want you to attempt to kill the North Korean Prime Minister and make it look like the United States Government did it and failed. And then, if you survive, to return home and wait for your next mission."

"What? That is suicide."

"Oh, you can kill as many of the bodyguards and support people you wish, but do not succeed in killing the Prime Minister; just make it look good and make sure it looks like the U.S. CIA did it. Use as many, or as few, of your people as you desire; just make it look good."

"How are we going to get into North Korea? We are not CIA or any undercover agency like that; my men do not have the training to pull that off. It will take time to plan and train for a mission like that."

"You have time, but you need to complete it within the next ten days, Mr. Monahan. Ten days is all we have to complete this. I have my reasons and that is all you need to know. As for equipment, you tell me what you need; and I will make sure you get it. You should have most everything already; however, anything you are missing I will get and have to you as quickly as possible. Oh, one other fact you need to know, that is the Prime Minister is going to be in Hong Kong for a secret meeting with my father. I will give you the exact location and time as soon as my operatives tell me. My father will be there; and if he dies then, I will be sad, but not overly, if you understand what I am saying, Mr. Monahan. The clock is ticking, Mr. Monahan. I will be staying at the Hyatt in Fargo if you need me. Just call, and I will arrange to meet with you. Goodnight, sir."

With that Soto stood, and he along with Tara walked out of the conference room and into the elevator. Minutes later, they were in the Bell Jet Ranger and flying to Fargo.

Chapter 22 Best Laid Plans Rarely Work

Eight hours after the firefight and extraction from North Dakota, Connie, Brian and Mona were sitting across from Josh Randal in a conference at CIA Headquarters. Davin's body had been delivered to the Walter Reed Hospital morgue. All during the flight back to Washington, Connie sat quietly considering how she was going to avenge her husband's murder.

"Okay Josh, Commander Green was not very explicit about the why we were suddenly and unexpectedly extracted from North Dakota. So now, it is your turn to explain; so, old buddy, what the hell is going on?" Connie questioned as soon as she entered the office.

Sitting across the table from Connie, Josh just sat and thumbed through the stack of papers in front of him without speaking.

"Well?" Connie piped in and looked at Mona and Brian confused as much as they were.

"Just wait, we have a guest coming that needs to be here," Josh finally said. "He will answer all our questions."

"Can you give us a hint at least?" Brian asked and then picked up his coffee cup and took a sip.

"No," Josh said and then stood and walked out of the office. "Be right back."

Minutes went by and finally Josh returned with Tony Sanford following close behind. Tony walked over to his half-brother Brian and gave him a hug.

"I am glad you are out of there, Brian. I was so worried," Tony said to his brother and then to everyone else. "Josh you can explain, if you would."

"No, sir; I cannot. Did you order the extraction?" Josh questioned.

"I did order the extraction," Tony Sanford replied.

"Why?" Josh asked again and still did not get an answer. "Okay, sir. Please, everyone, I will bring you up to date; and maybe President Sanford will tell us why he jumped the gun and ordered the extraction." Josh paused looking seriously at Sanford and not understanding why he would order the extraction early. "What you are about to hear is of course classified 'Top Secret', and we will add a code word to that to compartmentalize it shortly," Josh started to say. As he waited for everyone to quiet down again, Sanford interrupted him.

"Connie, I am so sorry for your loss; and we will do everything in our power to get that son of a bitch," Sanford said and paused for a second to let her speak.

"Thank you for your concern; but I want to kill him. He is mine, and I will pull the trigger on him. Is that clear?" Connie challenged, and then continued quickly, "I need to be reinstated in my position with the FBI, immediately." She was a professionally trained FBI agent, one that could hide her emotions, which she was only partly doing right now. He could see the hatred in her eyes; she wanted out of this room to kill George Monahan.

"Consider it done," Sanford said and then to Josh, "Make it happen, Josh."

"Now, let me say a few things which may help you understand why I ordered the extraction. When I asked Josh to put together an extraction team, I had also asked DHS to put together a backup team. DHS assembled a team headed up by Commander Green and ordered them to stage themselves outside the compound. I had Randal's team under the command of Kyle Lasko join up with them bringing the team up to ten. Six from DHS and four from CIA," Sanford started to say, and then stopped and looked at Connie only partly understanding what she was going through.

"I made an executive decision to shut down your missions and pull you out for several reasons, none of which the CIA has knowledge of. I ordered Green to go in, my decision, nobody else's.

It was based on multiple pieces of intelligence information, and I felt it was time to end this. The situation around the world has changed a lot in the past few days. North Korea and China are about to start a war, and we are the target. We have gathered intelligence from various sources indicating that the Prime Minister of North Korea is massing his troops along the border. There is more; we intercepted traffic suggesting that Rocky Soto and his son, Horatio, are in bed with the North Koreans and ISIS. That is a very nasty combination of people, to say the least. Our sources tell us that ISIS is in the market to purchase weapons of mass destruction and Mr. Soto is the person that is supplying them. His son has ordered Monahan to attempt to kill the North Korean PM and make it look like our CIA was responsible. Not sure how that is going to play out, but he has paid Monahan to make it happen. Our sources also have told us that the PM will be in Hong Kong in the next couple of days to meet with Rocky Soto. He will be staying at the Ritz-Carlton, Presidential Suite on the top floor which has access to the heli-pad on the roof by way of a private stairwell."

"Okay, wow; we knew about the WMDs, Soto and ISIS, but didn't know about the assassination attempt," Josh commented in defense of his organization.

"Thought you might have caught wind of that from your agents in the field. The bottom line is we need to keep China out of the picture completely. If they get involved, well, the results will be that we will probably have to learn how to speak Chinese. In addition, somehow we need to stop Monahan from his attempt without implicating the CIA. I am open to suggestions," Sanford concluded.

"Mr. Randal, I am not a CIA, I am Secret Service and report to my brother; so, with that stated, what do you want me to do?" Brian asked.

"You have a choice, Brian, one, help out the CIA; or two, fold back into the service and work, maybe in the White House. You are one of the best agents on the staff and it goes without saying that I trust you with my life more than some of the other agents," Tony stated before Josh had a chance to speak. "Josh is that fresh coffee in the pot?"

"Yes," Josh replied just as a light knock on the door interrupted them. "Just a second," he said to the group and stood up to answer the door. At the door was his secretary, Meredith. She handed him a sealed envelope and then turned and left. Josh closed the door and returned to his seat before opening the envelope. "Damn, you guys need to know this. According to our source, Horatio Soto did show up to the compound via helicopter. He met with George Monahan, the second in command, only because you were not there, Brian; and he has ordered George to send a team to Hong Kong to attempt to kill the Prime Minister, but fail in doing so in order to make it look like we did it. The 'we' being 'us', the CIA."

"But we already know that, Josh," Brian said quietly.

"Yes, but this confirms that the meeting has taken place and it is in motion. The earlier message only stated the plan that Horatio wanted to do, which he had discussed with our undercover operative."

"Damn, cool idea, what better way to piss off the North Koreans and have them shoot several nuclear missiles at us in retaliation," Connie commented. "Did your operative give a time frame as to when this is supposed to take place?"

"Yes, within the next ten days. What do you have in mind, Connie? You can sit out of this if you want. In light of what has happened, I would recommend it."

"No way, I want to kill that son of bitch that shot Davin and tried to kill me. You can have the rest, but I know it was Monahan and he is mine," Connie stated flatly.

"Well, since you are thinking Brian and Mona should fly off to Korea, maybe we send along some support to assist them in stopping Monahan and his assassins," Sanford said.

"The only problem I see in that is if we fail, we would have real agents on site to solidify that we had a hand in the attempt," Josh responded.

"Yes, but we will not fail. We can't fail; the safety of the free world lies in the success of the plan," Connie countered.

"But as some would say, 'the best laid plan goes to hell when the shooting starts,'" Tony stated shaking his head in disagreement.

"I have to agree with Tony. No matter how much we plan, and yes, our track record has been pretty good; but I guess the bottom line is, if they succeed, then we become a target. If we intervene and fail, we become a target. If we succeed and are able to cover our tails well enough and not let Monahan and Soto win this round, then we are targets only because there was an attempt that failed either because we intervened or not. We as a nation are still a target for North Korean and possibly Chinese nuclear missiles."

"Then it is settled, we intervene; but we don't wait until they go. We hit them here at home and take them out before they get a chance to execute their plan," Brian stated looking around the room at the rest of the members of what could be a botched attempt. "I need to go back in and see if I can divert the effort."

"Yes, you and Mona need to go back in. Stephanie will coordinate from the Fargo office. Mr. President, can we get another team ready to go in, maybe a larger group than the one we used to extract?" Josh asked.

"Do you think you can stop them before going, Brian?"

"Honestly, no. Monahan is a pretty formidable soldier and once he sets his mind there is not much that can change his mind," Brian stated, "But."

"There is always a but. What is the 'but' with this one, little brother," Tony asked.

"The 'but' in this is who is in charge, Monahan, me or this Soto fellow. If it is Soto, then stopping him may be impossible; but I will try, up to the point of killing him myself," Brian stated seriously. "Stephanie can you take Chilly with you to Fargo and keep her safe?"

"It may come to that. Okay, let's figure out how we are going to get you two back in without raising a red flag," Josh said and then looked at Connie.

"I will take care of Chilly, don't worry about her," Stephanie agreed.

"Brian, you and Mona leave in one hour; we will get you in before the sun comes up," Josh said and turned to Stephanie and added, "You leave in the morning for Fargo."

"Just get us to the edge of the property; I have a way in that Monahan does not know about. The same way we walked out. We just need the same weapons we left with; and well, we still have the same clothes on so that is not a problem."

"Then it is settled, make it happen, ladies and gentlemen," Tony ordered.

"One final thought, what do we do if we fail?" Connie asked, and then stated, "Remember, Monahan is mine!"

"Go to North Korea," Tony responded.

A knock on the door interrupted the conversation again.

"I told Mary we are not to be disturbed, what is up now?" Josh questioned and then pushed the intercom button. "What is it, Mary?"

"You have two more visitors and they insist on being let in," Mary said.

"Who?"

"The Pierce twins."

Without saying another word, Josh pressed the button under his desk to unlock the door and let Josh and Amber Pierce enter the office.

"Josh, Amber I am very sorry for your loss," President Sanford said as he stood and greeted the kids.

"We want in, no matter what it is. We want in to avenge our father's death," Josh stated with conviction. Amber stood beside him with a stern look and agreed.

"Josh, I will handle this. I am trained and prepared to take him out," Connie said as she walked over to her two children.

"No, mom, we are going and there is nothing you can say to stop us. Dad trained us in the use of weapons and more. He wanted us to be ready for anything and this is the one time we have to disobey you, mom. We are going with you or on our own. Short of putting us in jail, you cannot stop us," Amber stated seriously.

"I will not stop you; but if you go, and that is a big if, you will follow my orders, no question or delay, understand?" questioned Connie, and they quickly agreed with the stipulation.

"I can't allow two children to do this," Sanford said as he cut in.

"You may be the president, sir, but he was our father and we are going," Amber spoke up.

"Damn Pierce stubbornness, okay, but your mom is right; you follow her lead and orders," Sanford finally agreed shaking his head in disbelief.

After the meeting broke up, Josh received another message from his contact, Tara Wong, on the inside. There was to be a secret meeting between Rocky Soto and the Prime Minister of North Korea in Hong Kong in four days. His contact said the meeting was to be held in the Presidential Suite at the Ritz-Carlton. Josh briefed Stephanie, Connie and the team leaders on this new information minutes after receiving it. Plans were changed to intercept Monahan and stop them in Hong Kong if Brian failed in North Dakota.

Chapter 23 Missing Personnel

"Moose, we have accounted for almost everyone," the young militia man reported.

"Who is still missing?" Moose asked as he looked over his list of possible men and women he had at his disposal to take on the suicide mission he had to complete.

"Mr. Forest and Vale, Henry Blackstone, Jeremy Von, the Pierce couple, and we believe, but are not sure, the partial body we found is the kid Silverstone. Not sure, still trying to find his head; whatever he was hit with blew him to pieces. We may never find all of him," he reported.

"How many are dead? And can you get me a list of the names so I can take them off the active list. Don't worry about either Pierce; I think I killed him, both left on that chopper."

"Yes, sir; here is the list of the dead. Shall we bury them up on the hill with the rest?" the young militia man asked although he thought it was a stupid question.

"Of course, where else are we going to bury them? Contact the local coroner, and have him or her come out and prep the bodies. And, before you say anything, yes the local police will want to know what happened; we will tell them that we were attacked by unknown hostile forces and in the act of defending our home these fine, gentle, persons died. But we want to do the right thing with them, so report it."

"Yes, sir."

"Now get out of here and find Forest and Vale, if they are still alive and here," Moose ordered; and then went about crossing off the twenty-two names of the dead and missing from the active list.

"Damn it to hell; we lost some good people today and for what? And now we have a mission to do for Mr. Soto that is virtually suicidal," Moose said to his lieutenant who just walked into the room where he was sitting.

"Sir, we have a problem?" his lieutenant stated as he walked into the office.

"What problem could be worse than what we already have?" Moose asked looking up at his lieutenant as he stepped aside to allow a man in a police uniform walk in followed by three more officers each carrying an assault rifle and wearing full SWAT gear.

"Officer, sorry, Captain Spoon, what brings you to our humble little ranch?" Moose said, knowing exactly why they were there.

"Heard you had a little run in with some unknown group; we came up to talk to about that. Any idea who they were? Maybe a rival group, or a government force of some kind? What are your thoughts, Moose?"

"How did you hear about our little firefight so soon. It just ended a couple of hours ago?" Moose asked.

"A little bird told me," Spoon responded, "What happened?"

"We are trying to figure that out, Spoon, but are at a loss for the moment. We have twenty-two confirmed killed by them; they took their wounded or dead with them, so we cannot account for their side. Whoever they are, they were well trained and equipped. They left here in two Super Blackhawk helicopters, and had two Apache attack choppers in support which leads me to believe they were government."

"Where is Brian?" Spoon asked looking around the room.

"We don't know; they may have come in to kidnap him and to retrieve two new arrivals."

"New arrivals, who newly arrived that I did not know about?"

"None other than Mr. and Mrs. Pierce; they are on your most wanted list I believe."

"Why the hell didn't you tell me about them? I could arrest you and your whole group for harboring criminals."

"Why start now? You know what we are doing here, Spoon; so, don't play coy with me. I know that Forest has had you and your boys on the payroll for months. So, cut me some slack. We were going to turn them over to you in a few days. May we talk in private for a minute?" Moose asked and Spoon turned and indicated to his men to step outside.

"Okay, look, right now we have twenty-two known dead, six missing and are still canvassing the compound for those six. This is a big place with a lot of hiding places; they could be almost anywhere. If they are here, we will find them. Now, what I need from you is a little cooperation; we have a mission laid on, and it will take some highly trained people to complete it. Have you anyone that looks oriental, Korean preferred, and has training in undercover work?"

"As a matter of fact I do; what is this mission?" Spoon asked being of the curious nature.

"We have been asked to attempt, understand attempt, to assassinate the Prime Minister of North Korea. It may be a suicide mission; but it will be our suicide, if we don't try. We are also supposed to make it look like the CIA botched the job."

"Interesting, to say the least. Okay, Hun is on the payroll and I will have him report to you this afternoon."

"No, I don't want to train out here, we have to complete this within ten days, so I want to pick my team and we will move to your police training facility and camp there while training, if that is all right with you, Spoon."

"Sure, I will make sure the officers that are not working with you will stay away from there for the next few weeks. I can tell them we are making some improvements or something and the facility is closed down."

"Good, we will assemble out there tomorrow at noon. If you have anyone else that would like to join in, have them be there too. For those that survive, I will make sure there is a large bonus for them; or for their family, if they don't."

"Noon, at the police training facility; I may be there for your initial discussion with your team, but will not interfere."

"That will be good too. If you can provide any equipment, or suggestions, that would be greatly appreciated too, Spoon. Now, get out of here so I can get this suicide mission put together."

"Later, Moose," Spoon said with a laugh and left the room to Moose and his lieutenant, who had sat quietly in the back of the room.

"Are you going on this mission, Moose?" his lieutenant asked.

"Do I look Korean? Yes, I am going. Can't leave this mission up to some bozo that can't find his ass from a hole in the ground. I need you too, so pack you bag," Moose said and then added, "We need to relocate this afternoon. I am afraid those bastards will return to finish the job."

"Who do you want?" his lieutenant asked.

"Here is the short list, if they are still alive, they go; if not, well, then we go anyway," Moose said and handed him a short list.

"There are only six names on this list," he questioned.

"Yeah, you and me, plus those six is more than enough. Besides, we will be getting Hun, and maybe one or two more from Spoon. This party is small, but we need a couple of guys to die with CIA creds on them to make this work right. So out of those six, pick two or three to die on site even if we have to pull the trigger," Moose said smiling.

"Okay, I will get the men packing up their gear; we can be ready to roll in two hours, tops," his lieutenant commented and then hurried out of the office.

"Hello," Moose said after pressing the answer button on his new cell phone. He didn't want one of the newest implanted ones, preferring to use an older small phone. "I understand; we will change to arrive in Hong Kong in two days. Make sure we have a charter flight for possibly as many as twelve, rooms in a hotel close to the Ritz, and a contact to get weapons."

After ending the conversation, he stared at his phone and then yelled for his lieutenant to come back in the office. After informing his lieutenant of the change of location to Hong Kong, he just sat there and thought. *'What the hell; is this guy trying to start a war?'*

Chapter 24 Out of the Dark

After their drop off at the southern side of the compound, Brian and Mona showed, the Major in charge of his return, the entrance, in case he needed to infiltrate the compound again.

Shortly after Brian's arrival at the missile base, he had located some old construction diagrams for the facility and discovered there was an escape passage from deep inside the base located near silo number ten. The passage was about two miles long. It ran from about a hundred and twenty feet below the surface up to an exit trap door just outside the fence area. He and Mona had checked it out and found that it still had electric lighting and was just as it had been left over sixty years earlier. It was originally designed as an escape route if the base was overrun; there were four possible exits on the surface, one for each major compass point.

After reaching Silo Ten, they exited and entered Silo Twelve where they knew the bodies of two militias were located. After entering, they sealed the door. Once inside, Mona was instructed by Brian to shoot him in the leg and hide the gun and flashlight. When they heard a rescue party approaching, they quietly waited.

"Hell, nobody ever comes down here, why are we even bothering?" the lead hunter questioned as they walked down another set of stairs going deeper into the silo.

"We are down here because Moose said to come down here and look for Forest, Vale and the other missing guys. I don't like this anymore than you. Look at all the footprints in the dust on the floor. This place gives me the creeps..." He paused because he heard a noise. "What was that?"

"Sounded like a woman's voice. Is this place haunted?"

"No way, man; but let's check it out, and get the hell out of here. Sounded like it came from over there," he said as he pointed toward Silo Twelve. They stopped to listen, and heard the voice again. "Yeah, for sure, coming from Silo Twelve; let's get it open and see what we find."

He pounded on the door several times before getting a response from the other side, a muffled voice asking for help. "That sure sounded female," the other hunter said.

"Let's get it opened and see what we have," he responded and then with much force they pried open the door and shined their flashlights onto the dirt covered face of Mona Vale.

"Hurry, Brian is hurt," she said; and when they entered, they saw other bodies lying on the cold floor. "I think they are dead. I could not find a pulse, but you may want to check."

One of the hunters bent over and checked the two other bodies in the silo and shook his head. "They are dead; how did you get in here?" he asked.

"Soldiers grabbed us and put us here; we resisted, they were killed, and Brian was shot. I guess they were planning to come back for us, but never did," Mona said quickly as the men checked on Brian.

"We will come back for them; let's get you and Brian out of here and to the infirmary," the lead hunter stated and then picked up his radio and attempted to call up Moose with no luck. "Doesn't work down here, does it?"

"Nope, we are over a hundred feet down under a hell of a lot of concrete," his partner replied as he helped Mona lift Brian to a standing position; he was semi-conscious and barely able to walk, but they were finally able to get him up the stairs after several failed attempts.

"He has lost a lot of blood; I tried to stop the flow with what I had," Mona said as she pointed to her bra wrapped above the bullet hole and a part of her shirt tied around the wound. Her shirt was torn around the bottom where her make shift bandage had been exposing her midriff.

Upon reaching a level where there were active phones, the lead hunter called Moose's lieutenant to inform him that they had found four of the missing personnel and they were heading to the infirmary with Brian and Mona.

"Great, I will let Moose know," the lieutenant responded, not letting on that Moose had left the compound several hours earlier.

An hour after recovery of Brian and Mona from the depths of Silo Twelve, he was sitting up in the hospital bay of the compound with a young medic stitching up his wound. After applying a local antiseptic and removing the nine millimeter round, he pronounced Brian almost as good as new.

"Thanks, sorry I don't remember your name," Brian said as the medic finished up the stitching.

"Bill Currumbin, from Australia, no worries mate," Bill said with a smile.

"Why are you here?" Brian asked being curious as to why a trained medic would want to work with this bunch of misfits.

"I was originally hired by Mr. Rothschild, but when he died I was asked by Mr. Clark to stay until they were able to hire some doctors and then decide if I wanted to continue. I am not like the rest of these men and women; I am only here to patch up anyone that gets hurt. I don't know if I should say this, but I don't believe in your cause, Mr. Forest," Bill stated, "I am here because the pay is good; and I haven't received my Paramedic certificate from the state yet. I was a medic in the Australian Navy, and they don't issue certifications for Paramedics for the United States, so I have to go back to school and pass the state test to get my cert. I need money to do that, which is why I am here; that, and this is the only place I can practice medicine without getting noticed by the law, to keep in practice, while I save up to go back to school. Is that a problem with you sir?"

"No, Bill, thanks for telling me. You can stay around, but try to stay away from the military types; don't fall into their ways. You may have noticed; they lost twenty-four men during a firefight, and I was shot and almost kidnapped. As for going back to school, when I get things back in order here, I will loan you the money to go back to class; you will have to promise to return here to work for me. I am going to follow through with Mr. Rothschild's dream, and I will need some good medics. Deal?"

"Yes, sir, deal," Bill agreed.

"When do classes start?" Mona asked before Brian could.

"The university has classes starting in about two weeks and is about 1000 hours of training for the Paramedic level and costs about $10,000; should take me a year to complete."

"And with the training and experience you already have, you should breeze through the course. Good, then it is settled. I will finance you; and you will work here in this facility once it is back on track."

"Brian, we need to find Moose and see what is going on," Mona suggested.

"Sure, thanks Bill. I will talk to you again soon; get the application for the school completed, and don't worry about the money. Let's go Mona," Brian said as he hopped off the table. "Oh, should not have done that."

"Be careful with that leg, Mr. Forest. Come back tomorrow, so I can change the dressing. I am usually here from nine to five every day and on call the rest of the time. I bunk just next door."

"See you tomorrow," Brian said as he hobbled out the door.

"Do you want a crutch or a cane?" Bill asked.

"A cane may help. Thanks," Brian said as he took the cane from Bill and headed down the hall.

"Moose, we located Forest; he and four others were locked up in Silo Twelve. Mona and Forest are alive; the other three are dead. Forest is in the infirmary getting patched up; he took a bullet in the leg. Said he would be up here as soon as he is patched up," his lieutenant said into his cell phone.

"Good, are the men almost ready to roll?" Moose questioned.

"In another twenty minutes, the trucks will be loaded; and we are out of here."

"Good, I want that place locked down tight. We may be back in a few weeks, and I want it to be ready when we get here. Once we close the blast doors, nobody should be able to enter without you or me to enter the proper code. What are we going to do with the doc?"

"He is not one of us, and would be a problem if we take him. Can't let him just go; he may talk. I really don't think killing him is smart. Maybe we should just lock him in and leave him till we get back; there is enough food and water to last several years."

"Good idea, I will make sure Forest is good with it, but go ahead and move him in there; explain to him it is for his safety and ours. If he has a problem with that, take him to the hill and plant him."

"Right," his lieutenant said with a smile. "I will handle it right now." He turned and almost bumped into Brian Forest as he entered the small office. Brian stopped the lieutenant from leaving by holding onto his sleeve. "Wait."

"Moose, did I hear you right? You are leaving and locking the place up with the doc inside?" Brian asked as he took the cell phone from his lieutenant and then sat in the chair across from Moose's desk.

"Yeah, don't want to kill him; and don't need him to interfere with our operation. If we vacant, he can stay here; he has everything he needs, food, water, television, and more until we get back. The three of us are the only ones with the code to open the door, so he will be safe. Any problem with that, boss?" Moose explained.

"Okay, but I don't want him killed. You can leave to do whatever you have planned; I am kind of stuck here with a bum leg. We will wait your successful return, Mona, me, and the doc. When do you leave?" Brian questioned, "And where are you going?"

"We leave in about an hour and are going to Hong Kong. Too bad you can't make the trip; it's going to be fun. Just the kind of mission I live for," Moose said beaming.

"What is the mission? I think I missed that briefing."

"We are going to set up the CIA on an assassination attempt on the Prime Minister of North Korea. Oh, we are not going to kill him, just scare the crap out of him, gonna be fun," Moose said as if he was telling a joke, laughing.

"Don't screw it up, the CIA and FBI are already on our ass and that little firefight proves they know we are up to no good and are probably on their way back here right now to finish the job," Brian said, knowing it was not a joke, and that he had failed on stopping Moose from leaving the compound.

"That is why we are locking up and leaving; now Brian, I would love to chat, but I have to go. Will you lock up for me, and stay inside until we get back?" Moose asked politely.
"Sure, can't do much more until this leg heals. Mona, let's go to our room and get a shower and some rest. Moose, stop by just before you leave, so I can lock up behind you. Okay?" Brian said. He handed the phone back to the lieutenant, and pushed himself out of the chair with some difficulty.

"See you in the morning," Moose said smiling and hung up the phone. He was glad Brian was not able to go. He would have been a problem during the raid; and he did not want to kill another boss.

As Mona and Brian walked down the hall toward the elevators that would take them to their suite, Brian could only think of how he would stop Monahan. Not knowing where he was located was only part of the problem.

Moose was taking the remainder of the men, only seven left out of the thirty-eight they had yesterday; and flying off to start a war. With these seven, Monahan, and whoever he picked up from Spoon, he would have enough to do the mission and leave a couple of bodies behind to make it look like the CIA did the hit.

Chapter 25 Firing Range

George Monahan and his small team met at the police training facility early in the morning. Spoon was waiting there with Hun, his oriental officer.

"Good morning, Moose. This is Hun Wan Lu, a native Mandarin Chinese speaker. He holds several high degrees in martial arts, and will follow your orders without delay for the right price."

"Welcome, Mr. Lu, as far as price, would a hundred thousand work for you, half now and the rest upon completion of the job," Moose offered.

"Very well, Mr. Monahan. I will not let you down," Hun Wan Lu said with a small bow and handshake.

"I'm glad you agree; let's get inside and plan this op," Moose said. He turned and entered the small workshop that the police usually used for training and planning for urban warfare.

"Good morning, gentlemen. This is Captain Spoon; he has agreed to allow us the use of this facility. And this is Hun Wan Lu; he will be joining us. His credentials are simple, a member of the local police force, ex-special forces, and well, the list goes on. Again, welcome. I will say right up front; if you feel you don't want to participate in this exercise, please leave now," Moose said. He looked around the room for any takers. Seeing none, he continued, "Good. As you can see there are only eight of us including Lu. Before I get into what we will be doing, I need to tell you that we are being paid very well for this job, a million dollars apiece. I hope that meets your needs. I will also tell you that some of you may not come back, this is as close to a suicide mission as you can get. Anyone want out now?"

"What is the job, Moose?" asked a middle-aged man in a dark red shirt, blue jeans and sneakers.

"Richard, we are going to pose as CIA agents and attempt to kill the Prime Minister of North Korea," Moose stated quickly.

"Wow, how the hell are we supposed to do that? Isn't he in North Korea," Richard asked as the chatter in the room picked up.

"Well, that is the easy part. He will be in Hong Kong in a couple of days, which gives us a few days to plan, train and then fly over there," Moose responded with a smile.

"Cool, never been to Hong Kong," Richard said.

"If you survive this mission, you will have been there and returned home rich. The PM is supposed to have a meeting at a fancy hotel in downtown. We are to meet with a Saudi by the name of Ali Sharmeri. He will supply us with whatever weapons we need. When we arrive, we will link up, get the weapons we need, and fake credentials showing we are CIA. I will scope out the hotel, and locate the best way to get to the PM. Four of us will do the attack with the rest of you as backup and to provide cover if needed. You will be placed around the hotel lobby and entrances to provide cover and to alert us of any unwanted visitors," Moose briefed.

"Who gets the joy of popping the PM?" a voice spoke up. "I get that honor; Lu will be with me along with two of you. I will decide, after I see how you handle yourself on the course Spoon has set up out here. The weapons we have here are the same as what you will get when we get there. We will fly over on a private charter and pose as business men on holiday. If you don't make it through customs or have a record somewhere that prevents you from flying internationally, I need to know now." He paused to wait for a reply; and after getting none, he continued, "You will not carry any weapons while travelling; and you will check in separately at the hotel I tell you. Don't do anything to attract attention to yourself. You are tourists looking to have a good time in Hong Kong. Understand? And trust me on this; if you're not having a good time in Hong Kong, you are spending too much time reading," he finished as he received a nod from everyone in the affirmative. "Okay, Spoon has your weapons laid out on the back table. Get your weapon, and meet outside in five minutes," Moose said. He then walked to the back of the room where he chatted with Spoon for a brief moment before heading outside.

"Spoon had a mock city at his disposal, that included a three-story hotel. That's what they had planned on using to practice entering the hotel suite. Based on the photographs he was able to download from the internet of the Ritz-Carlton, they were able to set up the mock suite almost perfectly to match the original. They were sure the PM would be in the Presidential Suite on the top floor. There would be a separate elevator to reach that floor, and the PM would have guards positioned at that elevator to prevent any unauthorized use.

For the next two days, Moose ran them through multiple scenarios, positioning the targets in various places within the suite. He had them standing, and/or sitting in the kitchen, living room, balcony, and bedroom. He also used four to six bodyguards with various weapons and skills to ensure he had every possible situation available. At the end of the second day, he gathered his men outside.

"Gentlemen, I have tried to throw at you every possible scenario that I could think of and with the help of Mr. Lu, I believe we are ready. Now get some sleep, we fly tomorrow. We will meet at the Fargo General Aviation terminal at six in the morning for our flight; please leave the weapons and go. I will see you in the morning," Moose said.

He turned to Spoon, and walked off with him toward the police cruiser parked beside the building. They finally shook hands before Spoon got in his car and drove off the facility. However, Monahan still wasn't sure he could trust Spoon and seriously considered killing him just to be sure they were not ratted on before leaving.

Chapter 26 Hong Kong

Two days before he was to meet with the Prime Minister, Rocky Soto arrived in Hong Kong after a long flight from Bombay, India on his private jet. He was tired and a bit disturbed. The eclipse was spectacular; but the upload of his software had failed completely. Rocky was especially upset that his attempted software upload that would have allowed him access to the world's secrets and banks, when and where he wanted to do so, had failed.

To top that off, the recovery of the nuclear warhead had not happened. During the process of bringing it to the surface, the shell, weakened from being in salt water for over twenty years, fell apart; and the core slipped out of the cradle and drifted down into one of the deepest trenches in the Indian Ocean. The average depth of the Indian Ocean, 12,990 feet, had made it difficult to raise the warhead. Since they were close to the Java Trench when the warhead had fallen apart, the core slid down the wall into the trench estimated to be over 24,500 feet deep. This made recovery impossible with the equipment they had. Rocky aborted the recovery and flew to Bombay and then on to Hong Kong.

The two Navy ships had finished their inspection of the *Bonaventure* and headed north to Rocky's second ship. They arrived after the warhead had been lost, and the crew insisted they were there working on a project for the University of Bombay, conducting a study of marine life in the area. Since there was nothing suspicious about what they were doing, the crew of Rocky's ship was left to continue with their studies. The U.S Navy had been deceived; there was nothing further they could do at this time. They were in international waters; and without any legal right to do any further search of these vessels, both Navy ships headed southeast to continue their normal patrol around Australia and the South Pacific.

Checking into the Ritz-Carlton, the largest and most beautiful hotel in Hong Kong, was a treat to any traveler. The hotel was world famous for its charm and catering to guests, no matter who they were. At various times, services had been provided for guests that ranged from Hollywood movie stars to heads of state from most every country around the world. When price was not a concern and you had a need or desire for privacy, solitude and things you could not get in just any hotel, you stayed at the Ritz-Carlton.

Rocky had reserved a suite and was given the key to a two-bedroom suite on the twenty-eighth floor. It wasn't a palace, but you could not get much closer to the amenities and plushness of the suite. Nothing was left to chance when dealing with the rich and possibly famous. Rocky was impressed and thought that he could easily get used to staying in a place like this.

"Room service, would you send up a bottle of red wine and a medium rare rib-eye steak with baked potato, no vegetables. Thank you," Rocky ordered shortly after settling in his room. Standing at the floor to ceiling window, he gazed out at the city below and wondered what exciting things were happening just beyond the glass.

Rocky wanted the extra time to relax; the past week had been very stressful, and he needed to wind down. Maybe he would request the company of one of the many beautiful escorts that frequented the hotel. He could afford the company; maybe he would get two. A nice massage after dinner and a little play in the bedroom would really relax him.

Unknown to Rocky was that his son and his new girlfriend, Tara, were getting settled in a room on the eighteenth floor.

"Tara, I need to get a shower, why don't you order us some dinner and then we can talk about what we will do with Moose when he completes his mission," Horatio said as he started to remove his clothes and head to the bathroom.

"What would you like?" Tara asked as she watched him take off his shirt.

"Something oriental, but not sea food, had enough in the islands," he said and then closed the door to the bathroom.

Tara picked up the phone, dialed room service, and at the same time sent a text on her cell phone to Josh Randal back at CIA headquarters letting him know her location. Josh quickly forwarded the text to Connie who was on board the company jet flying to Hong Kong.

Moose and his team of ten were at the Harbour View Place just down the street from the Ritz-Carlton. The accommodations were far above anything his men had previously experienced; and the men were really enjoying their time to relax in the luxurious rooms. Each of the ten men had their own suite, paid for by Horatio in advance.

"Wow, this is great. This place is a mansion compared to the missile base we have been staying in. Maybe we should extend our stay and spend more of Horatio's money," Moose said to his lieutenant as he sipped on a bottle of Tsing Toa beer he retrieved from the mini fridge. "Help yourself to a beer or something; Horatio is paying for it. Why not indulge."

"No thanks, boss, but I need to take a couple of the boys and find the contact for the weapons. Should be back in a couple of hours," his lieutenant said and started for the door.

"Okay, have them delivered to your suite and make sure they all work; get enough ammo to start a war," Moose said with a chuckle, making a joke; yes, they were going to start a war. "Get it, start a war, we are going to start a war."

"Yeah, yeah, I get it! Just continue to drink your beer; I will be back shortly," his lieutenant said and left.

Three hours later, there was a knock on his door waking Moose up from his near drunken stupor. Standing up on rocky feet, he shuffled to the door, looked through the peep hole, and saw his lieutenant standing in the hallway.

"Come in, young man. What did you get?" Moose said after he opened the door and staggered back to the sofa.

"Our benefactor came through big time," his lieutenant said and handed Moose a pearl handle stainless steel custom Colt Forty-five semi-automatic pistol.

"Wow, this is nice; bet it cost him a bunch. Magazines?" Moose asked and held out his hand to receive a loaded mag, slid it into the weapon, and jacked a round into the chamber. "Smooth, but not something the CIA would use; too flashy. But, I will keep it anyway. What else did you get?"

His lieutenant described the weapons and explosives he acquired, and suggested that they have a meeting of the team in the morning to distribute the weapons, so each man could ensure he knew the proper function and had enough ammo to complete the job.

"Good idea, get some rest; that flight over and a couple of beers nearly kicked my ass." Moose suggested. "Oh, tell the boys to rest tonight, no women; tomorrow night, or after the hit, we can play."

The next morning, all of Moose's men were sitting comfortably in his room waiting to hear the plan. Earlier Moose and his lieutenant had walked over to the Ritz to do a recon of the hotel. They located exits, and learned the Presidential Suite was located on the forty-sixth floor and had a private elevator to get to it. The forty-sixth floor was the top of the hotel; above that was a helicopter landing pad, large enough for two helicopters. Both men had dressed in business casual clothing in an attempt to blend into the clientele of the hotel.

"Okay gentlemen, after a short but successful survey of our target hotel, we have come up with a plan to infiltrate the hotel and successfully complete our job." He stopped speaking for a moment to take a sip of the dark black cup of coffee he had ordered from room service and then continued, "Hun, I am so happy that you joined us; you will play an extremely important role in this operation. I will come back to you in a moment. The rest of you are going to be tourists, I hope you brought your cameras."

"Didn't plan on shooting pictures, boss, just shooting guns," one of his men said with a chuckle.

"Then I suggest that all of you go out and buy an inexpensive camera and hire a good looking escort or two to drag along with you. That will help in your cover story as rich business men out having a good time in Hong Kong. Here are a couple of local magazines with listings for escorts, and you can also see what is on the web. You will need them for the next two days. If you can't find what you want in there, I saw more in the little store down on the corner, but those magazines have some pretty hot ladies' pictures in them."

"I like that," another of the team piped in just as there was a knock on the door.

"Now who the hell is that?" Moose said. He walked over, peeked out the spy hole, and then opened the door to allow Tara Wong to enter. She was disguised as an old lady, just like she was when he met her at the compound four days earlier. "What can I do for you, Miss Wong?"

"I was sent over to drop off this," Tara said in a squeaky little voice and handed Moose a small envelope. "He thought you might need a little extra cash to get supplies," she said and then turned to leave, but stopped and turned back to Moose. "He asked if you would come to his hotel in an hour to discuss your plan. We will meet you in the lobby lounge."

"Sure, one hour, lobby lounge in the Ritz. I will be there," Moose replied. He took the envelope from her, closed the door, and walked back into the living room.

Moose opened the envelope to see five banded bundles of one hundred dollar bills equaling about fifty thousand dollars. Quietly he said, "thank you", as he thought of how she may have looked when younger. *'She was a looker at one time, but now bent and old. Older than my mother,'* he thought to himself. If he only had seen her without the disguise, he would have been greatly surprised.

"Okay, I have cash to pay for your hookers," he said holding up the envelope, "Have your girls tonight; and get your cameras. The weapons are in Duke's room, so we will meet in his room, ah, room 1807, just down the hall, bring a carry bag to get your weapon and ammo at two. Do not let your hooker see them. Now get breakfast, your camera, and order up your hookers. We will go over the plan at two this afternoon; don't bring your hooker with you."

Minutes later, he and his lieutenant sat alone in his suite.

"Good idea about the girls and camera, that should help us blend in," his lieutenant, Duke, said and then picked up his coffee and sipped.

"Yeah, I figured what the hell, some of these guys may be dead in two days and well, grabbing a little ass before will boost their moral; and besides it does help our cover story as business men on holiday," Moose commented and felt proud of himself.

"So what is the whole plan, boss?"

"Here is my idea..." Moose outlined his plan and took suggestions to make it better; he wrote some notes on the pad in front of him. They finally came down to a plan that had a ninety percent chance of working.

"I do believe that will work. Now get out of here; I need to get on the web and find me a hooker. If that Tara was a bit younger, I would have loved to tap her. She was probably pretty hot when she was younger, but she is way past her prime now and I am not into old cougars," Moose said as his lieutenant was leaving, not knowing the Tara he saw was in full disguise as an aging old woman.

"Looks can be deceiving, you know, she may be great in the sack. But face it, Horatio is no spring chicken either, he must be at least seventy, maybe older."

"Maybe, now get yourself a lady," Moose said and closed the door. He walked over to his laptop computer, sat down, and contemplated his next move.

Chapter 27 Putting on the Ritz

"How did it go?" Horatio asked when Tara returned to their room.

"Fine, he took the money and smiled; didn't ask any questions. I need to get out of this outfit; this hair is itchy. Where did you get it, some horse factory?" Tara complained as she walked across the room heading for the bathroom to remove her makeup and clothes. Because of the limited power on the one and only holographic projection device he had decided that using Hollywood style disguises would be best. Use of the projector would have to be when they didn't' have to stay in disguise for long periods. And when used, Horatio was the user, not Tara.

"I purchased that at the finest wig salon in North Dakota, cost all of fifty bucks. Live with it," Horatio teased.

"No wonder, it's horse hair. Says right here on the label. After I get changed, we are going shopping for a new wig. I am not wearing that one again."

"Okay, don't get so snippy. I will buy you a good wig, but it has to look like that one or your disguise will be blown."

"Sure, baby," Tara said and then came out of the bathroom in only her bikini panties and tiny bra, walked over to the dresser and pulled out a pair of jeans and blouse. "I will be ready in a few minutes. This makeup takes some time to remove, but it is good stuff used by Hollywood." When not in disguise as an old woman, Tara was a five foot four inches tall, Oriental beauty, with coal black hair, ample breasts, and thin waist, who looked great in a bikini.

Four hours later, Horatio and Tara made it back to their room with two new wigs and a bag full of theater makeup. To ensure their safety, they decided to go with various different disguises. The plan was to be in the Ritz when Moose and his team made their move on the PM. He also wanted to make sure his father was in the hotel when it happened.

Sitting at the desk while Tara put her new purchases away he heard a quiet vibration. "Is that your phone or mine?"

"Must be yours, mine is off," she replied as she pulled her cell phone from her pocket and looked at it. She read the text message that just came in and immediately pushed the button to erase it. Horatio was standing behind her.

"Not yours," he said and grabbed for the phone, causing her to drop it to the floor. He pushed her away and picked it up, tapping the screen he retrieved the last text. "Who is this texting you?"

"I don't know. Ever since we arrived, I have been getting these strange texts. I just delete them and hours later another one comes in," Tara confessed, looking shocked.

"Meet me at 4 in lobby," Horatio read, "Sounds like a guy trying to make time with you. Did you give out your number to anyone?"

"No, why would I?" Tara looked him directly in the eye as she spoke; she was an excellent actor, as well as a superb CIA agent.

"I don't know, you are a beautiful woman when not in disguise; maybe someone hi-jacked your number and is stalking you. Turn it off. No, better yet, I will keep it; and next time I will respond and we will find out who is doing this," Horatio said and then pocketed the phone. His suspicions were that she was not who she said she was, and he needed to watch her closely.

"Let's get some dinner, the restaurant off the lobby looked good. And I am dying for some Italian," Tara suggested.

"Tall, dark and handsome," he teased, and then said, "Give me a minute to put on my disguise, and you should too. We did check in as an old couple, and I don't want the hotel to get the impression that we are not who we say we are."

"Yeah, good idea. I will be ready in about twenty minutes. Call down for reservations," Tara said and then went into the bathroom to become an old woman.

It took both of them twenty minutes to change into their new disguises and head down to the restaurant. After a nice dinner, they walked around the hotel for a few minutes looking for any sign of Moose and his team. Horatio did not know everyone on Moose's team, but knew how to spot professionals. He did spot several men that looked suspicious with young beautiful Chinese women on their arms, obviously well paid women. But that did not prove they were part of the hit team.

"Horatio I'm going up to the room and change into something a whole lot more comfortable. Are you coming up?" Tara said after the walk through the atrium. "This is sure a beautiful hotel."

"No, go on up; I will be back shortly. I have a few things to take care of. Actually, let's go into the bar and get a drink before you go up. Remember, you told Moose to meet us in the lobby bar," Horatio suggested.

"Yes, I forgot, there is a table near the entrance where we can watch for him. And besides, a little night cap will loosen me up; and maybe we can have some action before the action starts," Tara said smiling.

"You tease baby, but I do need a drink," Horatio said and they walked over to the lobby bar. When the waitress, a cute little Chinese girl in a pair of tight black slacks and white blouse, came over, they ordered drinks and sat back to relax and wait for Moose.

Across the lobby Connie, Josh and Amber were checking into the hotel. The rest of her team would come arrive during the next couple of hours. Connie and Amber would share a room while Josh would have his own.

"Room twelve forty-two, Miss Pierce and young Mr. Pierce is in twelve forty-three," the clerk said. "Your bags will be in your room when you get there."

"Thank you, sir," Connie said and then turned to her children. "Let's get settled and then come down for some dinner, that Italian place over there looks good."

"Good for me, mom," Josh said and then picked up his carry bag and they followed their luggage to the elevator. The bell captain pressed the button to call the elevator and then rolled the luggage cart toward the elevator for luggage saying he would meet them upstairs.

Horatio, Tara and Moose were sitting in the lobby bar when Moose saw Connie and her team walk in and head toward the elevators. Their eyes met.

"Holy shit!" Moose exclaimed when he saw that she saw him sitting there. He stood and immediately reached under his jacket and started to pull his pistol out.

"What the hell are you doing, Monahan?" Horatio asked quickly not seeing Connie across the lobby.

"That bitch Pierce, get down!" Moose yelled and then brought his pistol up and fired.

Connie saw Moose pull his weapon, pushed her kids out of the line of fire, and then dove behind a chair just as a bullet slammed into the pillar next to her head. Reaching for the pistol in the small of her back, she pulled it out and glanced at her kids and Charlie who dove for cover as several more bullets slammed into the front desk. Guests were running for cover all over the lobby; luckily, no one was hit. Moose was firing wildly not taking time to aim.

"We have to get out of here, NOW!" Moose yelled at Horatio and Tara. Both were down hugging the floor. Tara pulled her weapon out and was about to shoot Monahan when Horatio pulled her back down to the floor.

"What are you doing, Tara? He is on our side," Horatio questioned as he started to crawl across the lobby toward the kitchen door.

"I wasn't going to shoot him," she lied and then said, "You go; I will back him up," Tara ordered and then slid up behind Moose. Horatio reached the door, slipped through it, and disappeared. Moose emptied his magazine of fifteen bullets and reloaded quickly. Tara ducked down just as several bullets hit the wall behind her and Moose.

"Need to leave. Cover my ass," Moose ordered.

"Cover your own ass," Tara said quietly and pointed her weapon at Moose but did not get a chance to pull the trigger when she was hit from behind by a bottle. Horatio stood in the doorway looking at Tara now lying on the floor.

"Kill her!" Horatio ordered, but instead Moose turned and ran toward the door where Horatio stood, and pushed him through. Both men ran through the kitchen and out the back.

"Monahan, go to your hotel and complete the mission. I am going to my suite and change. Now go," Horatio ordered when they stopped briefly at the staff service elevator. "Why didn't you kill her?"

"I was out of bullets," Monahan replied and then turned and exited the building.

Connie and her team were still in the lobby when the police showed up. They had some explaining to do; but once they showed them their credentials and answered a few questions, they were free to go to their rooms. The police allowed them to keep their weapons since they were CIA and on an official mission, tracking down a known terrorist. Just before leaving the States, Josh had issued CIA credentials to both of the kids so they could move freely around Hong Kong.

Tara had been on the floor unconscious, but recovered quickly in spite of a large bump from the blow to her head.

Fortunately, before the police found her, she had been able to sit up and slip her weapon into the waistband in the small of her back. Hopefully, she would not be patted down. Having a weapon and no credentials on her would prove to be a problem. She explained to the police that she was having a drink in the bar when the shooting started; and was hit from behind by someone. She answered a few other questions for the police and then headed for the elevator where she stepped in right behind Connie. As the door closed, she looked at Connie and the kids and smiled.

"Miss Pierce, I heard about Davin, great loss, I am so sorry," Tara said with her back to Connie.

"What, who are you?" Connie questioned immediately and reached out to turn Tara around. Tara turned and faced Connie with a tear in her eye.

"I work for Davin and Josh. My name is Joanne Morgan, but known here as Tara Wong. I am working undercover as Horatio Soto's girlfriend. It took me a long time to work my way into his life, but I think my cover has been blown. I need your help."

"Davin told me about you Miss Morgan. Said you are one hell of an agent," Connie said. "And Josh sent me a text saying you were here working undercover."

"How can we help you?" Josh piped in.

"I need to change my disguise, but can't go to my room. Just before I was hit from behind, Horatio had left the bar. But I think he is the one that hit me; and if I am not mistaken, before I passed out, I heard someone say, 'Kill her.'" Tara said almost pleading. "If I don't leave now, I will be dead before morning."

"Room twelve forty-two, you can stay with me; I have a two-room suite," Connie said; and as the door opened on the twelfth floor, she and the kids walked out. "I have some clothes that should fit you. Amber, you don't mind sharing do you?"

Forty minutes later, Joanne Morgan, aka Tara Wong, walked out of the second bedroom wearing skinny jeans, a black blouse and platform boots. She looked like a woman of the evening with the heavy makeup she had applied and a new blonde wig. Joanne had completely transformed herself from the old woman she was in the elevator to a sexy lady of the evening.

"Sorry for the way I look, but around here it is easier to blend in as a call girl than a little old lady," Joanne said as she walked over to the sofa and sat down.

"Miss Morgan, would you teach me how to apply makeup like that?" Amber asked blushing a little.

"Amber, I don't want you to look like a hooker. But that wig of mine does look better on you than it did on Amber," Connie scolded.

"Mom, that wig looked just fine on me. But the makeup will really help me blend in," Amber responded. "I just want to learn. You have taught me a lot; but if I am going to be in the family business, I need to learn as much as possible. Don't you agree, Miss Morgan," Amber countered.

"First, call me Joanne; and if it is okay with your mom, I will teach you as much as I can in the time we have," Joanne answered and then received an okay from Connie.

"I am not sure I want you to be in the family business, but can't stop you if that is what you want," Connie said and then poured herself a drink from the mini bar. "Technically, you are already a member of the CIA; Josh gave you creds and a license to carry a weapon; Davin, ah... taught you and Josh too much. But I am happy that he did; this is an unsafe world and you need all the protection you can get, especially as beautiful as you are."

"I could use one of those, if you don't mind," Joanne said and walked over to the bar.

"Sure, help yourself. Josh put us on an unlimited tab to get this done, so blend in," Connie agreed. "Amber, you may as well have one too. You are of age, and besides over here the legal drinking age is, I think, around fourteen."

"Thanks mom, but a beer would do me just fine. And thanks for the compliment," Amber said as she pulled a Tsing Tao from the fridge.

"What's the latest about this op? We have been on a plane for the past eighteen hours," Connie said as she sat down on the sofa with her drink.

"Monahan is in the Harbour View right next door. He has nine soldiers with him and recently received a lot of artillery and explosives. I dropped off an envelope with lots of cash. What he plans on doing with that, I don't know. It was a gift from Horatio. They are in rooms on the fifteenth floor; Monahan is in fifteen-ten and his troops are in nine down to one all on the fifteenth. The PM is due in tonight via private jet and is to be in the Presidential Suite on the top floor. Meeting is scheduled for noon tomorrow. We haven't seen Rocky Soto yet, but know he is here. That's all I know. And thanks for taking me in, you saved my life," Joanne stated to relate her story.

"Can't let you get killed, Davin spoke very highly of you and only wished he were here. Have you made contact with Josh recently?" Connie asked.

"No, we were supposed to make contact at eight tonight, but Horatio took my phone," Joanne said.

"Use mine, it is secure," Connie said and handed her the phone.

"Thank you," Joanne said as she took the phone and then asked, "Speed dial?"

"Oh, star one," replied Connie.

Later that evening, three black Chevy SUVs pulled into the underground garage of the Ritz-Carlton and stopped next to the Presidential Suite private elevator doors. Eight bodyguards climbed out of the vehicles and immediately secured the area around the vehicles and the doors. They pushed the button and inserted the special key card that opened the doors of the elevator. After checking that it was empty, four of the guards stepped inside and pushed the button for the suite. They arrived in the Presidential Suite moments later and ensured the room was empty and safe. Two of the guards returned to the garage to get the Prime Minister while the other two stayed in the suite. As soon as they arrived and indicated the suite was safe, one of the bodyguards opened the back door of the middle SUV and the Prime Minister slipped out and into the waiting elevator.

Three minutes later, they were all in the suite. The Prime Minister looked at his five men and three women and smiled. "Thank you, four of you can stand down; the rest of you remain on watch. I need to get some rest before the meeting tomorrow." Those were the only words spoken from the time they arrived in the garage. The bodyguards acknowledged with a nod, and then four headed toward the adjoining suite specifically designed to house bodyguards for all types of dignitaries. Keeping all bodyguards close was a must when traveling in foreign countries; and since the Prime Minister of North Korea was a prime target for most every country in the free world, he did not want to take any chances.

At the same time, one of Monahan's team with his expensive hooker hanging on his arm spied the three SUVs entering the garage and followed at a distance to make sure the PM was actually the one getting out of the SUV. With his new digital camera, he stood his hooker against the supporting pole and instructed her to do something sexy while he snapped a few pictures. After he succeeded in capturing a picture of the PM getting out of the SUV and into the elevator, he took her hand, and they walked back out onto the street and faded into the nighttime crowd.

Chapter 28 Wish You Were Here

"Josh Randal," he said when he picked up his secure phone.

"Josh my old friend, how the hell are you?" Joanne said over the secure line.

"Doing fine, Joanne. Are you there with Connie and the kids?" he replied.

"Yes, we are in Hong Kong, as you know; but I wanted you to know my cover was blown with Horatio Soto. Don't know how he found out, but he did; I had to scoot out of there with nothing but the clothes on my back. Connie has supplied me with some new clothes, and I did, of course, change my disguise. Much to young Josh's hormones, that boy is growing into one good looking stud. If only I was younger or he older."

"Whoa, little lady. Don't go messing with my godson. He may be of age; but, well, if he is like his dad, you don't want to go there, trust me," Josh cautioned.

"Oh, not to worry, big brother. He is cute and young, but not exactly my type," Joanne teased.

"Hey, I am not your big brother, just your boss," Josh shot back.

"Oh, you are 'big brother' to millions of people and you know it, Josh," Joanne quickly replied. Joanne and Josh loved to banter. They were very close, and this bantering was an essential component of their relationship; fortunately for Josh, his wife, Stephanie, and Joanne were also close. Although Stephanie did not understand the bantering at all, she tolerated that part of Joanne's relationship with Josh and loved Joanne like a sister.

"Okay, so you are safe with Connie. What's the plan?" Josh asked.

"Well, we have some agents watching the Ritz; that is where the PM is staying. Oh, and we are staying there too. Hope you don't mind the added expense, but we figured being in the same hotel would be best. Anyway, we have a couple of agents in the lobby keeping an eye out for Monahan, but so far no luck. However, we did have a bit of a scare in the lobby a couple of hours ago."

"Do I need to ask?" Josh said.

"No, Horatio and I were having a drink in the lobby bar, both of us in disguise, when Monahan came in and sat with us. We were discussing his plans when Connie and her team walked into the lobby and Monahan saw her. Immediately he turned and opened fire, almost hitting her. Lucky for Connie old Monahan reacted too fast and his shot went wide. Connie and everyone in the lobby dove for cover and two of her men returned fire. Horatio ducked and ran for the back of the bar looking for a way out. I saw an opportunity to stop Monahan and was about to take it when Horatio struck me in the back of the head. I knew he suspected I wasn't who I pretended to be; and when he saw me raise my weapon, he assumed I was going to shoot Monahan. Actually, I was going to deflect the shooting by firing a couple of shots at the agents with Connie, but Horatio didn't see where I was aiming and assumed, I guess. The next thing I knew Monahan had his gun pointed at me; why he didn't fire, I don't know. When I saw him running out the back with Horatio, I decided to get the hell out and joined up with Connie."

"Is that the whole story?" Josh asked.

"Yep, and I am sticking to it!" Joanne replied with a smile.

"Okay, put Connie on for a moment."

Josh talked with Connie for a few minutes, hung up the secure line, leaned back in his chair, and thought to himself, *'This is getting crazier by the minute, what the hell is going to happen next?'*

Just as he was deep in thought, the secure line rang again. He looked at it for a minute before picking up the handset. Only a handful of people had this number and the security device needed to talk on it, Connie, Davin (now deceased), Tony Sanford the President, the Vice President, Director of the FBI and Homeland Security along with a few other high government officials. The list was small for a reason; there were only certain people needing to contact the Director of CIA and he liked it that way. So, he wondered, who is calling now?

"Josh Randal is not available right now; he is out cleaning his weapons. Please leave a message at the tone and he will return..." Josh started to say, but was interrupted by Tony Sanford.

"Very funny, Josh. But we have to talk, seriously," Tony said quickly.

"Sure, sir. Should I come to your office?" Josh asked.

"No, open your door, and I will come in," Tony said and then hung up.

Josh stepped out of his office where he found Tony. "Come in, sir. I didn't know you were out there; and by the way, how did you call my secure line? No, don't tell me. If I know, then that tells me we have a problem," Josh said without much thought before he looked at his secretary smiling behind her desk while she pointed to the secure phone on her desk. "Oh, yeah, I forgot we put that there. Ah... Come in, sir."

Tony Sanford and two of his advisors stepped into CIA Director Josh Randal's office and sat down across from his desk, not even waiting for Josh to offer a seat. Josh closed the door, walked over to the credenza, and said, "Sir, would you care for a drink, coffee, water, soda?"

"Scotch, if you don't mind," Tony said quietly and then looked at his two advisors. After getting a nod from both, he added, "Make that three."

"Scotch it is, sir," Josh said as he picked up the bottle of twelve-year-old single malt Scotch, one of his favorites, reserved for only himself as well as special guests. He gave the cheap stuff to most everyone else.

"Thank you, Josh. And when are you going to quit calling me sir? We have known each other since I worked over in the FBI."

"When you have finished your second term, sir." Josh replied grinning.

"Look, we have a problem and need your assistance," Tony said after receiving and taking a sip from the glass.

"How can I help? The CIA is at your service, but you already knew that. What is the problem?"

"As you know, North Korea has been rattling their sabers again; and all indication from NSA is that they are looking for a fight. We have been attempting to reason with them, but that S.O.B. running the country is a royal pain in the ass; and, I believe, is just a little short of a full house, if you know what I mean."

"Yes, we have been monitoring the situation over there for years, as you know. Recently we had to pull one of our top undercover agents out when her cover was blown. Almost lost her. She is now working with Connie Pierce on the Rocky Soto case and is in Hong Kong," Josh said.

"That's good, but do you have anyone else in country that is supplying information and can get close to this maniac?" Tony asked between sips.

"Yes and no. We have four more operatives in country and they are working on getting as much information out as possible, but no they are not in as good a position as our female op. She was, well, one of the PM's girls. And from what I was told, he is a sadistic bastard, mistreats his women, and makes them do things that are against their nature. She had survived, but barely."

"Her loyalty will not be forgotten. What about the others? Can they get closer?"

"One young agent, a very pretty female is determined to get close; she has a chance, but it is risky as we learned from Joanne. If the PM likes her, she will move up to the palace and hopefully get some good intel. If she fails, she may be killed; but she understands the risks and is willing to make the move."

"Give her orders to make the move; and if she can get alone with the PM, well, I don't like giving orders like this, but this one needs to be done. Take him out," Tony ordered. "Make it look like an accident; I don't want to sacrifice her, but he needs to be gone."

"It will be done sir. Is there anything else?" Josh asked.

"Yes, if the other three can assist or do it before she gets into harm's way, then make it happen." After pausing, he then raised his glass and asked, "One more for the road?"

Chapter 29 Gunfight in the Ritz

The Ritz-Carlton was the most expensive luxury hotel in Hong Kong and provided service to its clientele that surpassed all the other hotels in the area. But it did cost; the average cost of the Presidential Suite for one night exceeded ten thousand U.S. dollars a night. Most amenities were included, food, drinks, and use of all the facilities.

The PM wanted to enjoy his stay. The first thing he wanted was a massage, but not from one of the girls the hotel would provide. Two of his bodyguards had additional duties as his personal masseuse.

"Victoria, would you please join me in my room, I need a massage," the PM said as he walked toward his private room.

"Yes, sir, give me two minutes to get my bag," Victoria said with a smile. She really liked the PM and especially enjoyed doing massages. "Do you wish Sue Lynn to join us?"

"Not tonight, just you," he said and then entered his room.

After lightly knocking on the door and without saying a word, the door opened and Victoria entered smiling. She had changed into a silk robe and carried a small bag containing lotions. The rest of the evening was pure pleasure for the PM and Victoria.

Rocky Soto sat in his room and scanned the television channels looking for something to help him relax. Even with over five hundred channels, he could not find anything that remotely interested him. He turned off the TV, walked over to the mini bar, and fixed himself a tall scotch and water. It was nearly midnight and he had a very busy day tomorrow. He downed his drink quickly, turned and headed for his bed. His plan to have a couple of ladies join him had changed; he was tired and decided not to indulge in a young man's fantasy, opting not to call for any ladies to spend the evening with. There would be time later for that.

Morning came, as it always did in a city that did not sleep, without any fanfare except on the city streets. The cars, buses, motorcycles and pedestrians flooded between buildings and moved to their next destination. Wherever that destination was, was anyone's guess.

The Prime Minister sat at his dining table and ate a small breakfast. His bodyguards were working in shifts; four would be on for four hours and then off, rotating to ensure the PM was covered twenty-four hours a day. Each male bodyguard carried two firearms; one was a Type 68 pistol equipped with a suppressor. This pistol was chambered for a 7.62x 25mm round which had high stopping power, but the bullet was not readily available outside North Korea, Russia or China. The second one was a compact sub-machine gun with a strap to hide it under their jackets. The female bodyguards only carried the Type 68. The VZ-61 Skorpion was the weapon of choice with a twenty round magazine.

At eleven o'clock, the Prime Minister looked around the suite and conferred with the lead of his guard force. Rocky Soto would arrive shortly and he wanted all to go well. Mr. Soto had some technology that he needed for his country and supposedly had a nuclear core to sell. He did not need the nuclear core, but was interested in the laser weapons that Soto could provide.

At precisely twelve o'clock noon, a chime sounded from the suite's intercom system. Victoria was standing closest to the intercom; she leaned over and pushed the button to respond.

"Yes," Victoria said in a very sexy voice.

"Mr. Soto, for my appointment," Rocky responded, not stating who he had an appointment with in case people could hear that the PM of North Korea was in their hotel.

"Mr. Soto, I will send down the elevator; please wait at the door," she said and then pushed the button to release the elevator to descend to the floor from which he had called. Inside the elevator, two of the PM's bodyguards were standing. Their job was to ensure Soto was who he said he was, and that he was not armed with anything, including ink pens.

"Mr. Soto, please step into the elevator and raise your arms," the tallest bodyguard requested when the elevator doors opened. He patted down Rocky, removed two ink pens and inspected both of them carefully. He returned them to Rocky's breast pocket before turning him around, smiled, and asked, "Are you ready for your meeting; is there anything you need before going up, Mr. Soto?"

"I have everything I need, sir."

His partner opened and inspected everything in his briefcase and turned it every way he could to see if there were any hidden compartments or dangerous traps. He found none and determined it was a cheap knock-off of a very expensive leather brief case. After handing the case back to Soto, he smiled, nodded to his partner, and pressed the button for the Presidential Suite after insertion of his key card into the slot.

A few minutes later, the elevator door opened onto the hallway outside the Presidential Suite and four other suites designated for support staff for whoever was in the suite. Rocky was impressed with the elegance of the hallway and only hoped the suite would be just as grand. He was not to be disappointed.

The tallest bodyguard stopped in front of the Presidential Suite's double doors and pressed the doorbell button.

"Are we clear?" Victoria asked in response.

"Yes," came the reply and the door opened to let the three enter. Both bodyguards stopped just inside the door, closed it behind them, and watched as Rocky Soto walked further into the suite. Rocky stopped short of the main living room to take in the view. He saw the Prime Minister sitting in an overstuffed leather recliner reading a small paperback book just around the corner.

"Mr. Soto, it is a pleasure to finally meet you," the PM said as he put down his book and stood, waiting for Soto to close the gap between them, a distance of about twenty-five feet. "Please come in and have a seat. Would you care for some lunch? I was just about to order, but decided to wait and see what you would like."

"Pleasure to meet you, sir. As for lunch, I am open to most anything," Rocky Soto commented and shook the PM's outstretched hand.

"Come we will sit on the balcony; it will be more comfortable and the view is spectacular," the PM said and led Rocky out the glass French doors to a large balcony overlooking the city.

Sue Lynn walked over and bowed gracefully, she knew he wanted to tell her something before he had to ask.

"Sir?"

"Order lunch for us, two bottles of red wine, and let's see maybe a couple of steaks. This place has wonderful meats, and make sure they are medium rare. Is that okay with you, Mr. Soto?" the PM asked.

"Fine, they do have excellent steaks," Soto agreed. "I had a rib-eye last night that you could cut with a fork, very tender and the flavor was outstanding."

"As you wish, sir," Sue Lynn said and then backed away to place the order.

In the hotel kitchen, the requested meal was being prepared with great care. Hun, a member of Monahan's assassination team had procured the restaurant's uniform and was preparing to pick up the order. The plan was to gain access to the elevator; and Moose, along with three others, would ride up and do what was required. They had tapped into the security video cameras to change the view the security guards would see, not realizing the view was a fake. This would allow Moose and his men access to the elevator to ride upstairs without being spotted before they attacked.

"Received an order for the Presidential Suite; is it ready?" Hun yelled at the chef, speaking Chinese. He knew that if you act like you are supposed to be there, most people would assume you were supposed to be there.

"Almost, keep your shirt on," the chef yelled back in Chinese. "Where is Janko?"

"He was tied up and they sent me. Problem?" Hun responded quickly in Chinese.

"No problem, just know they will search you when you get in the elevator. So, leave anything extra you have on the table over there and I will see that you get it when you get back," the chef said as he lifted two large plates and placed them on the cart along with two bottles of very expensive red wine and an assortment of other items. "Now go, they are waiting and they want it hot."

"Right, on my way," Han said and wheeled the cart toward the service elevator. Looking to his right, he saw Moose and three of his compadres standing just behind a wall near the elevator. Hun pressed the call button and waited.

"Yes," Victoria said into the intercom.

"Room service with two meals," Hun replied.

"What kind of meals?" Victoria quizzed, as she looked at the video monitor of the elevator doors, only seeing Hun with the food cart.

"Two medium rare steaks and two bottles of wine, the wine is at room temperature and the steaks will be too if we wait too long," Hun responded in English since she spoke to him in English, and he could not speak Korean.

"Understand, sending the elevator down now," Victoria said and two bodyguards entered the elevator and started down to the kitchen level.

The doors opened at the kitchen level, and Hun stared at the two bodyguards. The tallest one signaled for Hun to enter. Just as he crossed the threshold, Moose pressed a button on a remote that caused the video monitor in the suite to see an empty hallway, from a pre-recorded video which Moose had made earlier in the day. He pressed another button on his cell phone and the monitors in the security office only showed an empty elevator. Moose and this team rushed over to the elevator before the doors closed and shot both bodyguards in the head. They were dead before they hit the floor. The hotel security team only saw an empty elevator as the doors closed. The microphones were also silent.

Without saying a word, Moose reached down, retrieved and inserted the key card, and pushed the up button for the Presidential suite level. The elevator started moving. It would take two minutes to reach the Presidential Suite floor and another three to complete the mission; the escape back down the elevator and out of the hotel would take another two. That was if everything proceeded as planned.

Meanwhile in the lobby, Connie and her team were approaching the elevators; their plan was to go up to the fourth floor, exit the main elevator, move over to the Presidential Express elevator, and go up to the suite. Her tech assured her that he could bypass the security in the Presidential elevator, and get them up to the proper floor. The other half of her team were landing on the roof. They would come down to the Presidential Suite via the stairs. Again, they had the electronic equipment to bypass the security. Upon arriving on the fourth floor, they waited for a couple of minutes for the elevator to return. When it arrived, they saw two dead bodyguards, rushed in and called the team on the roof to move in fast. Moose had already gone up and was about to strike.

Seconds after arriving on the top floor, Moose and his team opened the elevator door to the hallway and looked out. Not seeing anyone, they quietly moved out and down both sides of the hallway. Moose did not notice that the elevator immediately started back down. Even if he had noticed, he would not have cared; his mission was about to begin, and he would not fail.

Hun rolled his cart toward the double door; he was sweating and worried about what was to happen next. After reaching the door, he looked at Moose and waited a second so Moose could get in place and charge their weapons. Moose had handed Hun a 9mm Smith & Wesson semi-auto pistol with two extra magazines. Hun hid it under a napkin inches from his hand. After getting a nod from Moose, he reached out, pushed the doorbell, and waited.

"Yes," Victoria asked when she heard the buzzer.

"Room Service," Han responded quickly.

"Where is Janko?" Victoria asked becoming suspicious.

"He stopped at his room to use the bathroom. Said for me to come ahead," Hun replied as he quickly made up this lie.

"Where is..." she started to say when Moose and three others rushed the door, and crashed through, knocked her against the wall behind her, and slammed her head hard. She slid down the wall unconscious.

Moose and his team took careful aim and shot the three other guards standing in the room. Suddenly, from out of the corner, four shots were fired from a suppressed weapon that immediately dropped two of Moose's men, dead.

Moose swung his Uzi toward the shooter and dropped him. Sue Lynn dove out the door to the balcony to protect her Prime Minister and shot from the hip. She took down a third member of the assassins. Moose ran into the room. Upon seeing her dive out to the balcony, he turned and fired at her. The shot missed Sue Lynn, but hit Rocky Soto in the shoulder. A second shot hit the Prime Minister in the waist just as the PM unfortunately stood to get out of the way. The shots had dropped both of them to the floor.

Sue Lynn fired again, but missed her target just as Connie and her team stormed into the suite. Hun turned and fired, dropping one of the CIA agents, dead. The third member of Moose's team was only wounded, so he continued to fire his pistol until it was empty. He successfully hit and killed another of Connie's team. Connie shot him in the head and then scanned the room for Moose. As she penetrated deeper into the suite, she could see the balcony with two bodies lying beside the sofa not moving; blood was everywhere. She could not see their faces; she only hoped that one was a dead Rocky Soto.

Moose dove for cover just as Connie pulled the trigger on her weapon that she had aimed at him. She missed when Moose rolled behind another sofa near an open door that he hoped would lead to the hallway. Popping a smoke grenade, he tossed it into the center of the room.

"Run, Hun!" Moose yelled into the headphone he was wearing. Hun heard the command in his earpiece and dove for the door, knocking over a CIA agent. The agent, thinking Hun was a hotel employee trying to get away from the gunfire, ignored him. Hun took advantage of that, shot the agent, hitting him in the shoulder, and then ran for the stairwell.

Moose took a chance and ran for the open door to the room next door. Connie continued to shoot, but did not hit her target. Seconds later, her second team burst into the room, saw the destruction, and pulled Connie back out of the suite in an attempt to protect her.

Sue Lynn continued to protect the PM and glanced over at Victoria lying on the floor beside the front door. Two CIA agents lay dead beside her and three of her team were lying in pools of blood; she assumed they were dead too. "Are you okay, sir?" Sue Lynn asked before climbing off him.

"Yes, who the hell are those people and how did they get past our security?" he yelled.

"I don't know, but I will find out," she vowed. "Mr. Soto, are you okay."

"No, I am not. I have a hole in my shoulder," Soto said quietly, grimacing in pain.

"Oh shut up! Sue Lynn, check on the others and call for a doctor," the PM ordered.

Moose and Hun escaped down the stairwell on the south end of the building. Connie's team had come in from the north stairwell, although she had also stationed a pair of agents in the south stairwell.

"Burns, Mike, check the south stairwell." When they checked on them, they found two of the bodies of their fellow agents. Hun was lying dead on the platform below her agents. Moose was gone, and he had succeeded in his mission.

Besides the four dead members of his team, Connie lost four of her own men and could not recover their bodies. They did not carry identification, but Moose's men carried forged CIA credentials and government issued weapons, well, stolen government issued weapons. The attack lasted one minute thirty seconds and everyone was gone except the dead within one minute forty seconds.

Connie's team was recovering in her suite on the twelfth floor. Amber was expertly patching the bullet graze that Connie had received and had not even known when she was hit. The other members were wondering how the hell Moose escaped so quickly. The first and most important thing to do was to locate Moose and take him down.

"Josh, Connie, we failed," Connie said into the secure satellite phone. After pausing for a moment for that to sink in, she continued, "What do you want us to do?"

"Run him to ground," Josh said and broke the connection.

Forty minutes later, a team of paramedics was patching up the Prime Minister and Rocky Soto. Victoria had awakened, after being slammed into the wall, and sat holding a bag of ice on the back of her head. She had just downed four Motrin to ease the pain. Sue Lynn was talking to the Hong Kong police describing the attack and giving as good of a description as she could. The suite had a camera aimed at the double doors that captured a clear shot of Moose and his four dead accomplices.

"If there is anything else you can add, Sue Lynn, please give me a call," the police detective said handing her his card. Due to protocol, the detective was not allowed to talk to the Prime Minister or even know he was there. Only Rocky Soto was allowed to speak and could not add much more than what Sue Lynn had already told them.

"Until we get to the bottom of this, please remain in town," the detective ordered.

"Of course, we cannot travel until Mr. Soto heals a bit anyway," Sue Lynn lied. She had already called for their private jet to be prepared for departure within the next four hours. She also called her contacts and requested a helicopter to pick them up on the roof in two hours.

"Mr. Soto, you understand that you cannot go with us; our next stop is North Korea. If you wish to continue with our transaction, we must solidify it in the next hour," the PM stated as he sipped on a strong shot of Vodka. He had grown to like Russian Vodka over the years and this one was especially good mixed with the pain killers the paramedic had given him.

"I understand..." Soto said and then outlined what he thought needed to be done. He said he was sorry that the nuclear device was now on the bottom of the Java Trench in the Indian Ocean, making it unavailable.

"Sir, the deal sounds good. Can you do it by a week from Monday?" the PM asked.

"I will make sure their defenses are down. You may launch at will when ready," Soto agreed. "I must be going now."

Chapter 30 Getting Away With Murder

Moose gathered the remainder of his team in his suite at the Harbour View and sat quietly while his men wondered what the next move would be. They knew the attack succeeded, but not without loss. Hun and three of the team were lying dead in the Hong Kong morgue.

"Boss, what are we going to do now?" Duke his lieutenant asked from across the room.

"We had some losses, but they don't know who we are; the boys had CIA creds on them, so the CIA will get the blame. Our next move is to get to the airport and fly out of here before they start looking for me," Moose said quietly, knowing that Connie got a good look at him and could bring some serious heat upon him.

"Why would they be looking for you? Did they take a picture, or can anyone identify you?" his lieutenant asked.

"Yes, that bitch Pierce was there trying to stop us. She failed, of course, but she got a good look at me; and, I think, one of the bodyguards is still alive who also saw me. You guys don't have to run; stick around and spend the rest of the money," Moose said and threw the balance of the envelope on the coffee table. "I have to leave. Contact our charter and tell them I will be there in two hours. When you leave, meet back at the compound in, let's say two weeks from today. Should be safe by then. I may not return, depending on what you tell me when you get back. I will be in contact. If you hear anything, relay it to Duke and I will stay in contact with him, or to Brian back at the compound. I will call him when I get back in the States."

"Roger that boss. Let's get out of here boys; the ladies are waiting," his lieutenant said and they headed for the door. After stopping, he turned, saluted, and said, "Be safe, boss."

That would be the last time Moose would see his men.

"Pack up boys; we are going to the airport. That will be the first place Moose will head. We need to stop him," Connie ordered; and then to Joanne asked, "Are you coming with us?"

"Yes, can't stay here; Horatio will kill me as soon as he sees me," Joanne said. "Do you have some extra ammo? I seem to have lost all of mine."

"Sure, nine millimeter. Good, we could use your help," Connie agreed. She paused for a second to answer her cell phone, "Yeah."

"This is Charlie; I'm down in the garage loading my gear in the rental and saw Moose racing out of here in a blue Honda SUV. I tried to get the license plate, but the lighting was too dark."

"That just speeds up our departure. Amber, tell Josh we will be back; stay here, and keep your gun handy," Connie ordered and then she and Joanne headed out of the door. She and Joanne took the elevator to the garage and jumped into their rental. Charlie had called the rest of the team and all but one was in the garage when she arrived.

"Where to?" Charlie asked as he climbed into the rental.

"Airport and fast. He is making a run. I don't want to lose him again," Connie ordered as Charlie pulled the car into the traffic outside the hotel.

"We have trouble, Connie," Joanne said from the back seat.

"What is it?" Connie asked.

"Cops just pulled out behind us, lights on," Joanne stated without emotion.

"Shit!" Connie exclaimed, "Step on it, Charlie. No, don't; slow down, and let's see if he wants us to pull over." She picked up her phone and called the rest of the team in the car that pulled out behind the cops. They were not speeding, just staying close behind the cops and Connie's car.

"We see them, Connie. What would you like us to do?" was the response.

"Nothing, just watch; Moose is heading for the airport and we are going after him."

"Roger that, consider it done. Be safe."

"Always, always," Connie said and then broke the connection.

The police cruiser closed in on Connie's car, but then accelerated and passed her.

"Wow, that was fortunate. How did you know?" Joanne asked Connie.

"Lucky guess. Now let's head for the airport. Don't break any speed limits; we don't want to be stopped with all this artillery on board," Connie ordered, as she looked down at the Colt automatic on her lap.

"Roger that," Charlie said and continued to drive. The police car was pulling away, but it looked like they were going to the same place.

"Do you think they are after Moose? That would be just about perfect," Blair said to nobody in particular.

"No, that wouldn't be good for us, or Moose, if caught," Connie said.

Moose had a good fifteen-minute head start, but the police had a lot of patrol cars, and his picture had been sent to every cruiser in the city. The cruiser that was in front of Connie had seen Moose exit the hotel garage and was in pursuit. He had radioed other officers for support. They were closing in on Moose and he did not know it.

Ten minutes from the airport, two cruisers pulled in behind him and two in front, boxing him in. But a desperate man will do things a normal person would not do. Moose was desperate, and was just about to take action. He reached over to the passenger seat, picked up his Uzi and racked a round into the chamber. Also on the seat were three additional fifty round magazines ready for use if needed. The two cruisers in front started to slow down forcing

Moose to slow also; that was their mistake. Moose slammed on the brakes, spun the car to the left, stuck the Uzi out the window and fired. He raked both cruisers with hot lead, and killed two of the officers causing the drivers to accelerate to get out of the line of fire.

After spinning the wheel harder, Moose was able to line up on the cruisers behind him. He fired, and killed another officer. He spun the wheel again and accelerated past the two cruisers that had blocked his way. He fired his Uzi into the side of the cruiser on his left until he was empty. The cruiser exploded when several of the rounds hit the fuel line. Moose accelerated to over eighty miles an hour on the crowded street, dodging pedestrians and other cars expertly. His Honda was not fast, but it was agile.

A mile behind Moose, Connie and her team saw the explosion and accelerated toward the fire. "He is almost to the airport, let's move it," she ordered.

Ten minutes later, Connie and her team pulled into the parking lot of general aviation and jumped out of the cars. They ran toward the open gate to the ramp. Two Hong Kong police cars were racing toward the parking lot behind them. They kept their weapons out of sight to prevent being arrested for possession of weapons, approached the gate, and started through.

On the far side of the ramp sat a Gulfstream VI with its engines spooling up and a large man running for the stairs to board. Suddenly he stopped. When he looked behind him, he saw Connie and her team running through the gate toward him. He looked at her and smiled, knowing that in a few seconds he would be on board his jet and taxiing out to the runway. Unless she took the chance to shoot him from over two hundred yards away with a pistol, he had made his escape successfully.

Connie saw Moose and started to draw her pistol when Charlie and Joanne stopped her.

"At this range you haven't a chance in hell of hitting him," Joanne said, "The cops will stop the plane from taking off."

Seconds later, with a big smile on his face, Moose climbed the stairs and closed the door. The big jet immediately started to taxi and within five minutes was rolling down the runway for takeoff. He was gone, for now.

Connie's team stopped running toward the jet as it started to move and just stared at it, hopeless in catching him and the Hong Kong Police were pulling up beside them, obviously with a lot of questions.

Joanne pulled out her newly acquired satellite phone, pressed speed dial number two, and waited for three rings until it was answered.

"Josh, we have a situation," she said when Josh Randal answered the phone.

A black Chevy SUV with Sue Lynn and one other of the PM's body guards pulled up beside the general aviation terminal. They stepped out and walked to the edge of the building to watch Connie and her team run toward a departing Gulfstream business jet. They were prepared to shoot and kill, but decided only to watch through the scope on the sniper rifle and not attract attention. The shot would have been easy for Sue Lynn, but would accomplish nothing in the killing of the CIA agents now being arrested by the Hong Kong Police.

Two police cruisers pulled up behind Connie's team and stopped. Sue Lynn had no idea what the police were asking. She had to report back and right now had no idea who the man was that boarded the jet, but she would find out and then extract revenge.

George 'Moose' Monahan entered the main cabin of the Gulfstream and saw an older, oriental gentlemen sitting in an overstuffed chair sipping a tall glass of wine. He did not recognize him as Horatio Soto. He was about the same age, but not the man who had contracted him.

"Who are you and why are you on my plane?" Moose asked as he walked toward the man.

"My plane and you are my guest, so please have some wine and take a seat, we are starting to move," the oriental gentleman said and then pulled his seatbelt tight. Moose sat down across from him, picked up the bottle of red wine, and poured himself a drink.

"Thank you. It is obvious you know who I am; but I, sir, am at a loss as to who you are?" Moose said and then took a sip of the wine. "I am normally a beer man, but this is mighty fine wine, sir," he said and then glanced out the window to see the police cars surrounding Connie and her team.

"They will be busy for a while, which allows us to make our escape more easily, wouldn't you say?" the old man said smiling.

"Yes, thank you. Now who are you?" Moose asked again.

"My name is unimportant, and after this flight you will not see me again. But I am your benefactor, I have provided your group with the money to grow and you have just completed the first of many missions for me. The next one is outlined in this folder. You met my brother, Horatio earlier; he is no longer available to meet with you, so you have to deal with me, now," the old man said, but still did not give the folder to Moose. "I will give it to you soon. But first, we need to toast the success of your mission. The Prime Minister is on his way back to North Korea. He has declared war on the CIA and the United States. Also, Mr. Rocky Soto was injured, but not killed. Too bad for that; wish you had killed him. But he will be useful in the future; he just doesn't know it."

"Where is your girlfriend?" Moose asked, hoping that he would catch this old man into admitting he was Horatio.

"Oh, you mean my brother's girlfriend; well, she is gone. I suspected she was working with the CIA and hoped you would have killed her in the bar. She escaped and is most likely hooking up with her CIA buddies already. We may or may not see her again, but she is a master of disguises so we may not even know if she is there or not. No matter, her days are numbered, along with her CIA buddies. That is part of your next job, Mr. Monahan. Kill her, her team and Mr. Josh Randal."

"Wait, how do you know about the bar?" Moose questioned suspecting he was talking to Horatio.

"I was there, behind the bar, tending it as it were," the old man said, not letting on that he was Horatio.

"You said, part. What other part of the job is there?" Moose asked.

"Read the file, Mr. Monahan and enjoy the wine; it is a long flight to Hawaii," the old man said sliding the file across the table to Moose. "I will not be staying with you. My plans require me to fly to, well, require me to be somewhere else in three days. I hope you understand. You mission went well; and your next assignment is to eliminate Josh Randal, Connie Pierce and her entire team. Failure is not an option, Mr. Monahan."

Chapter 31 What Would a Super Hero Do?

Spending the night in a Hong Kong jail was not on Connie's dance card. She knew that once the Hong Kong Police started asking questions, they would be detained allowing Monahan, a clean escape. The jet had already faded into the clouds over the city. Checking for a flight plan would help them in knowing where they were headed, but even that could change during the flight.

A middle-aged detective stepped out of a black unmarked police car, walked over to Connie's team, and smiled through perfect, extremely white teeth before saying a word. He just stared and looked like he was deep in thought, slowly shaking his head as if he just discovered a clue that had eluded him for months. He stopped in front of her team, and signaled for his officers to stay back with their cars, so he could speak freely with Connie's team.

"Mrs. Pierce, I presume?" He finally said looking directly at Connie. He paused for a moment, turned to Joanne and said, "And Miss Wong, or should I say Miss Morgan."

Connie and Joanne looked at each other in surprise that this detective knew who they were, but neither said a word in reply or acknowledgement.

"And I assume these men are with you. We know who all of you are and have been watching you since your arrival," he continued without waiting for any acknowledgement.

"Then you know you just let a criminal escape in that business jet," Connie finally said pointing to the Gulfstream Business jet that had just faded into the clouds.

"Yes, we know that too. But don't worry we have his plane on radar and have contacted your Navy to see if they can track it to its destination and maybe send a couple of fighters up to follow. But that may have been too much to ask of your Navy. Would it not? His flight plan says Hawaii, but, well, we shall see where he actually lands in a few hours."

"Track, yes; fighters, probably not," Joanne said before Connie was able to reply.

"How do you know all this?" Connie asked quickly.

"All your questions will be answered in due time, but for now let's just say we have a great working relationship with your boss," the detective stated and then continued, "Oh, where are my manners, I am Detective Captain Jon Wynn, Hong Kong Intelligence Agency." He held up his credentials for all to see.

"Pleasure to meet you Detective Wynn," Connie said holding out her hand for his in return. "Why are you here?"

"Please, let us go inside where we can be comfortable and talk."

"The terminal, or your office?" Joanne questioned.

"Privacy is required, so my office would be best; we are just off the airport property. Miss Morgan and Mrs. Pierce, would you care to ride with me? Your men can follow us to the office. Just give me a moment to dismiss these officers," Wynn said and then turned and walked to the parked patrol cruisers and spoke with the officers for a moment. He returned to Connie's team seconds later. "Shall we go," he said and turned to walk back to his car. Connie and Joanne followed close behind after instructing Charlie to follow.

Twenty-five minutes later, they were sitting in a very plush conference room on the fourth floor of what looked like a normal business commerce center. The lobby had a receptionist, a bank of elevators, a coffee shop, two small gift shops and a bank, not a bit unlike ones you would find in New York or Los Angeles. They had been led to one of the elevators that required a key card for access and then whisked up to the fourth floor and escorted to the conference room. Not a word was spoken during the ride over or until they were comfortably seated in the conference room.

"Would you or any of your team need the use of the facilities? They are behind that door right there, no need for an escort. Also, would any of you care for a drink, water, tea, coffee or something a bit stronger?" Wynn asked as they entered the room.

"Would love something cold," Joanne answered and most of the team agreed.

"Beer?" Wynn suggested.

"That would be perfect, if you don't mind," Joanne replied.

Wynn stepped over to the credenza and picked up a phone and ordered beer for all and a Scotch and water for himself.

After the drinks arrived, Wynn sat at the head of the table and sipped his drink watching everyone at the table before he spoke.

"Mrs. Pierce, as I mentioned at the airport, we have a close working relationship with your boss, Mr. Randal. He informed us of the operation you were about to undertake and asked if we would back your team up if need be. As it was, your team was very efficient and did not require backup. I'm very sorry that Mr. Monahan escaped capture, but rest assured he will be captured. His plane has been confirmed to be on course to Hawaii and I am sure Mr. Randal will have a team waiting for him at the airport."

"What about the North Koreans?" Connie asked. She was disturbed that her team would not be in on the capture.

"Ahh, that is another problem that we are hoping to stifle shortly. It seems they are a bit ticked off at the attack; rightly so, and they have dispatched a hit team, as it were, to eliminate Mr. Monahan and, sadly to eliminate you. His associates were killed in the attack along with a couple of your men. We are very sorry for your loss. The local police are on the scene collecting evidence and removing the bodies. Your men will be returned to your country after they have completed their investigation. This cannot be helped. I hope you understand. I have been informed that three of the dead were carrying CIA credentials and several had no identification at all. I assume your men were the ones with no creds and the others were very good forgeries to make it appear the CIA had made the assassination attempt. Am I correct in that assumption?" Wynn asked and then stopped to take a sip of his drink.

"None of my team would have had their creds on them," Connie stated.

"As it stands right now, you and your team are on their radar also as being accomplices to the attack, not trying to stop it, but part of the overall plan. And, more importantly, they believe the United States CIA planned the attack. The presence of two of your agents' dead at the scene does not help your case as well as three with credentials proving they were CIA. That is why I stepped in at the airport with my men. The North Koreans had a team at the airport and were about to take you out. You were in their gun sights; and if I had not intervened, you would most likely be dead now."

"We did not see any one at the airport other than you."

"Trust me when I say 'they had you in their sights', two shooters and two observers. We did see Sue Lynn, one of the PM's top assassins, watching you as you ran after Monahan. The only reason she did not fire was, we believe anyway, that my team showed up just in time," Wynn said bending the actual truth just a little to be sure that Connie understood the seriousness of the situation.

"That is very interesting, Detective Wynn. So, what do we do now? We need to get after Monahan; and you are telling me that the North Koreans are after us too. How are we supposed to get that part stopped without causing a war?" Connie asked.

"Well, war is going to happen; the North Korean Prime Minister was wounded and has disappeared. Shortly after the attack, two helicopters landing on the roof of the Ritz, picked up passengers and departed. We had positive identification of Victoria, his other female bodyguard leaving with him. Sue Lynn along with three others were also seen leaving the hotel following you. We followed her, and that is when we intervened. We assume he has returned to North Korea with the plan on attacking the United States in retaliation to the attack on him. He has already issued a threat and orders to prepare for war."

"Holy shit!" Joanne commented and looked over at Connie with a question on her lips, but Connie asked first.

"What would a super hero do now?" Connie said quietly, just as there was a knock on the door. Wynn stood, opened the door a crack, and stepped back to allow the two at the door to enter. Josh and Amber walked into the room followed by a well-dressed, oriental woman.

"Josh, Amber what are you doing here?" Connie asked. She quickly stood and hugged both her children.

"Mrs. Pierce, I had them picked up and brought here. We felt that for their safety they needed to be away from the hotel. I hope you don't mind," Wynn said quickly.

"I don't mind. Just glad they are safe," Connie answered. "Now, what?"

"My people will escort you to the airport where your company jet is waiting. From there, you will fly to Hawaii to meet up with some more of your countrymen and capture George Monahan," Wynn stated.

"What about our stuff in the hotel?" Joanne asked, "Well, I don't have anything there, but..."

"All your luggage is heading for the airport as we speak," Wynn replied. "We leave in thirty minutes; is there anything you require before leaving?"

Chapter 32 Which Way Did He Go?

Eighteen hours after Connie and her team left the offices of the Hong Kong Intelligence Agency and bid Detective Wynn farewell and a thank you, they were landing in Honolulu, Hawaii in a private CIA owned business jet. The CIA had no authority to operate within the confines of the United States; they were walking on egg shells just being here with weapons.

As their jet pulled to a stop, Connie glanced out the window to see three SUVs pull up close to the aircraft's wing and stop. Three men and one woman stepped out of the SUVs and stopped at the bottom of air stairs that were being lowered so the passengers could exit the aircraft. Connie and Joanne were the first to deplane and were greeted, at the bottom, by a member of the local Hawaii Five O, Lieutenant Valerie 'Val' Lake.

"Welcome to Hawaii, Miss Pierce. I am Lieutenant Valerie Lake, call me Val. We were notified of your arrival and are here to assist you in 'your off the books' operation," she said showing her credentials and then introduced the rest of her team. Connie in return introduced her team.

"What's the plan?" Connie asked.

"First, we get you off the airfield and to a safe house; and then, well, then we should have more information about your target and can make a plan to capture. Let's go; load your equipment in the vehicles and climb aboard," Val said, stopping as she started to turn and said to Connie and her kids. "I am really sorry to hear about Davin. He was a good friend; we had worked together on several of his less discrete jobs."

"Thank you, Miss Lake," Amber said and looked at her brother standing tall next to Connie. He was not saying a word, but had the look of revenge in his eyes. He wanted Monahan dead, not just captured. The same feeling ran through Connie and Amber, but they did not show the seriousness of the need for revenge that he had.

After a short drive, the SUVs pulled into an underground parking garage and stopped.

"We have rooms for all of you on the second floor, and I know what you are going to say, 'How can this apartment building be a safe house?' The answer is simple; we own the building. Now let's get unloaded, and I will check in with HQ for updates on Monahan," Val said as she and the rest of the teams started to unload everything.

"Damn, I'm tired; with all the technology man has created over the years, why haven't they created a faster way to travel, maybe something like a transporter or even a time machine," Amber commented as she, Josh, and Connie settled in their three-bedroom apartment on the second floor. The rest of the team had similar apartments on the same floor. The plan was to get a little freshened up before meeting with Val in a conference room located on the top floor in an hour.

At precisely an hour later, the team met with Lt. Lake in the conference room as directed. After getting something to drink and a sandwich from the buffet that was laid out for them, they took seats and waited for Lt. Lake to tell them what they needed to know.

"I trust your rooms are satisfactory," she started and then after a short pause continued, "Mr. Monahan arrived at Kahului airport on Maui a few hours ago. We are not sure where he went from there; my man lost him in traffic. He could still be on Maui; or, there are several options. He could have chartered another smaller plane or boat and flown to another island. We are hoping he is still on Maui. If so, we will locate him."

"Okay, what is your suggestion as to what we should do? We can't just sit here and wait," Connie said.

"Well, that is what you may just have to do. We also heard that several agents from North Korean have landed in Honolulu and may be looking for you. We have identified two of them as Sue Lynn and Kim Lee. Both are suspected assassins, but we have no proof of that," Lake stated.

"That is just great! We are cooped up in here; and the North Koreans are out there chasing down the killer of my father. We need to get out there and stop him before they do," Amber cried out.

"Hang on, Amber; we will get our chance, sooner than you think," Connie replied quickly.

"Mom, he killed dad and we need to kill him," Josh finally spoke up.

"We will; we will!" Connie agreed.

"There will be no killing on our islands, kids. We will arrest him as soon as we find him and turn him over to the FBI and prosecution. Understand!" Lake said in a stern voice.

"Okay, no killing, for now," Connie responded quietly, looked at her children, and received their agreement.

"Look, we will find him, if he is still in the islands," Val said.

"If those two are known assassins, why don't you arrest them?" Josh asked.

"Wish we could, but they have not committed any crimes on the island; and we don't have any proof they are here to commit a crime. A flaw in our laws prevents us from just rounding up people on a just because."

A light knock on the door interrupted the conversation. Lake stood, walked over to the door and opened it, took a folder from the man at the door, closed the door, and turned back into the room.

"Good, we just received an update on the status of the Koreans. They have linked up with some friends. We have identified six agents and it does look like Sue Lynn and the one they call Victoria are both here. They are teamed up with, well, you don't need their names right now, their pictures and bios are in the folders I will give you."

"Is this the same Sue Lynn you said was a highly efficient assassin? And before you answer that, what about the others, Victoria and the rest of her team?" Joanne asked. "I believe I ran into Sue Lynn a few years ago during a mission to North Korea."

"She was once the head of the Secret Service, rank of colonel, according to the report Mr. Randal sent us," Lake commented.

"Must be her, but that would make her almost fifty years old," Joanne stated.

"Age in the Orientals means nothing. She may be getting older, but she may also be getting much bolder. Which is why she is heading up this team, I suppose. She has nothing to lose," Connie answered.

"Age means a lot to us Orientals. Look at me, I am Japanese and do I look like I am growing old gracefully?" Joanne asked feeling slighted. She, being the old age of forty-two, could and had passed off as a young twenty-eight-year-old. She had Horatio fooled from the minute they met.

"Joanne, you look beautiful," Josh piped in, smiling at her.

"Thank you Josh, but growing old is not for the faint of heart, believe me. If it were not for the make-up, I would look my age. But thank you for noticing," Joanne said with a smile.

"We are getting off track; Joanne, you are growing old gracefully," Connie said and then added, "And you don't use much make-up, except to go undercover in disguise."

"Just enough to hide some of the age lines," Joanne replied with a small chuckle.

"Ladies, both of you are beautiful, can we get back to the matter at hand. I would like all of you to remain here at the resort; take advantage of the pool, bar and food service. Everyone here works for Five O and are armed," Lake said, thinking that both of those women were still beautiful at their age. It was unfortunate that Joanne thought of herself as being a little over weight at a hundred and fifteen pounds and not nearly pretty as others thought of her.

"Pool and bar?" Amber said, "Where?"

"On the roof, it is a pool bar," Lake said pointing up.

"I didn't bring a bathing suit. Is there a place nearby where I could get one?" Amber asked.

"Yes, I will have one of my officers escort you to the store down the street that sells bathing suits," Lake offered.

"Good, I would like to go too," Josh said, thinking thoughts he shouldn't be thinking for a young twenty-year old, but his hormones were really starting to take hold. He had a beautiful mother and an equally beautiful adventurous sister, but he also had thoughts of the older women in the room, Joanne and Lieutenant Lake. Seeing either or both of them in a bikini would be very nice and boost his ego. He should have his chance of at least seeing Joanne later today in the pool.

"Amber would you pick up a nice suit for me and maybe Joanne," Connie asked.

"Sure, you and I are the same size; Joanne, give me your preference and size and I will get something for you too," Amber agreed.

"Good, now can we get back to business? We have a criminal to catch and a war to hopefully stop," Lake said and then passed out folders with the North Korean agents' information. A knock on the door interrupted them again. Lake stood and opened the door. "Good, come in."

A tall, African American, in a black silk suit, white shirt and dark blue tie stepped into the room, and closed the door behind him. "Thank you, Detective Lake," he said in a booming deep voice.

"I would like to introduce you to Senior FBI agent, Alfonso Lakota. He will be taking lead on this operation. Everything, and I mean everything, needs his approval before we proceed. Al, would you care to speak to the CIA team?"

"Sure, since you have no jurisdiction while on U.S. soil, the bulk of the operation will be handled by my team with Lake's as backup. Your team, Miss Pierce, will be able to accompany her team during the take down. As long as you are on U.S. soil, it has to be done this way; otherwise, we could have a serious political problem. Your boss, Mr. Randal, has approved; and, actually, he called both of us to assist in this. We will use this room as our operations and meet every day at eight in the morning and again at nine in the evening to go over the day's progress. I don't expect everyone to be here, but do need you, Mrs. Pierce and Morgan at a minimum."

"Only one question, how much longer are we going to sit in this room?" Josh asked feeling restless.

"Just a few more minutes," Connie replied and placed her hand on his arm to reassure him.

"Okay, I get it; you are tired, pissed off, and wanting revenge. You will get what you want soon; but first, let us find the S.O.B," Lake said and then added, "This meeting is over; get some rest; we will inform you when we get any leads."

Chapter 33 War Is No Game

"Mr. President, our latest information tells us that the North Koreans and China are preparing for war. We have to assume we are the target," the National Defense Secretary stated in the President's morning security briefing.

"What are the indicators?" President Tony Sanford asked from across the coffee table. This has always been a casual meeting in the Oval Office with the heads of each major department present. Enjoying coffee, pastry and conversation while discussing world events and making decisions that could change the world seemed easier in a relaxed setting. Today was no different from any other morning, except the tension was a lot higher and the real possibility of war was on the horizon.

"There are a lot of indicators. First, and foremost, the Korean Prime Minister was attacked by a team that has been identified as agents of the CIA. How do we explain that, Mr. Randal?" the director of NSA, Walter Kline, stated and was interrupted by Randal.

"What the hell is that supposed to mean, Walter? Yes, we had a team on site attempting to stop a team being led by George Monahan, a very crazed individual, being paid by sources unknown," Randal fired back.

"Okay, you know all about that; so, second, their ICBM sites have a lot of activity, fuel trucks, personnel and all the heat signatures from each site is off the scale," Walter continued.

"What are we going to do about it?" Sanford asked.

"Until we get some more information as to their intent, I don't believe we can do anything short of putting our military on alert and maybe prep our defenses," General Whitmore stated, but he did not sound very convinced that was the way to go.

"General, I do believe we need to rise the DEFCON level and put our forces on alert. Admiral Foster, alert your naval forces of the

DEFCON change and move your Boomers to within firing range of North Korea and China. I do not want to start a war; but I will end it, if need be," Sanford ordered, "If, and I have to emphasize if, if they launch, we will retaliate." While he paused for a moment before continuing, he looked around the Oval Office at his attendees wondering how they were going to prevent war.

"Would you four please leave the room for a moment, we have a few items to discuss that is above your clearance level," Air Force General Brady said pointing to four of the lower level members of Congress and the Senate. Without saying a word, they first looked at the President for approval; and after getting a nod from Sanford, all four left the Oval Office and closed the door behind them upon leaving, taking their coffee and pastry with them.

"Okay, gentlemen and lady, I asked them to leave because we need to discuss the possible use of the Star Wars defense system. First, as the representative of the Air Force and the controller of the Star Wars laser system, I need to bring it to the table once again," General Brady started and then stopped to see the reaction from the President.

"The what? I thought that was just a pipe dream from a bunch of geeks that never went further than the drawing board," Sanford questioned, staring at the General.

"Sir, I want you to know right now, it is fully functional, and we can depend on it to protect our country?" Brady replied with a smile.

"Fully functional, why the hell haven't I been informed on this before now. Who authorized it? When did you launch it? I need information; and again, why haven't I been told we have a lethal weapon floating around our country in space?" Sanford insisted.

"Plausible deniability, sir. If you didn't know about it, you could not answer questions from reporters that might have gotten wind of it. We kept it a secret to protect you," Brady replied.

"I understand that, but what about when and how?" Sanford asked again.

"Sir, it was launched over thirty years ago and only the sitting president at the time knew about it; and he only knew because he authorized its construction and launch. We have kept it on the back burner, as it were, and only bring it out now because of the situation with North Korea," Brady replied. "We tested the system extensively in the lab and on practice targets after launch and placement in space. I am fully confident that we can take out any incoming missiles," General Brady continued.

"All bull shit aside general, will you stake your life on that assessment?" Sanford asked quietly, not getting a warm fuzzy feeling about the comment.

"Sir, ah, yes I would. But keep in mind, it has been up there for over thirty years; and, ah, I will have to have the technicians run tests to ensure it is up to one hundred percent. The last space mission did make a brief stop at two of the satellites and updated the software and some hardware. They also tested it on a couple of out of service satellites with success."

"So you can't guarantee it will work one hundred percent," General Whitmore, of the U.S. Army, asked looking over at the Air Force General.

"No, but, sir, I will have a positive answer for you by noon tomorrow," Brady agreed.

"If it isn't one hundred percent, I will also need an estimate on how long it will take to get it back up to speed. If it means sending a crew up to fix it, then make it happen. The safety of our nation may depend on it," Sanford stated. "War on two fronts is not something I think we can handle if we have to put troops on the ground. Combat and support troops are at an all-time low, thanks to our previous administration and their budget cuts. The idea that technology will win over strength is not my idea of protection. We may have to use the Star Wars satellite laser defense system even at a reduced capability."

"How many Star Wars satellites do we have up there anyway?" Sanford asked.

"There are four, sir. And with the ground units that you already know about, it gives us the edge we need to defeat any aggressor," Brady commented.

"Being an old Army guy and not knowing much about space ships other than what I see in the movies, please enlighten this old dog as to what the hell this Star Wars thing really is," Whitmore asked looking a bit confused.

"Star Wars, named after the movie, is a high tech, laser system designed to target and destroy any targets that threaten the safety of the United States and her allies. The system was designed in the late 1990s, built, and finally launched in 2004. It had been tested and proven accurate and reliable, but that was then. Even with periodic testing, they were not completely sure the system could stand up to heavy use. The idea for the satellite laser system was based on the Hollywood movie, *Star Wars*, and the *Death Star*'s use of a high tech laser to destroy planets. The system in space over the United States consisted of four orbiting satellites controlled from five control sites located around the country. Each site could operate independently, if need be; or coordinate between each other to defend the country. The main control center was located deep in the site known as Mount Weather; the others were in Oregon, Arizona, North Dakota, and Georgia." General Brady said smiling.

"Wow, with those and our ground forces, the enemy should be shaking in their boots," Whitmore said with a laugh.

"Well, only if they know about it," Sanford added, "And right now only those related to the project know it even exists. Let's keep it that way, okay."

It was early that same Friday morning and almost seven thousand miles away on a small island in the middle of the Pacific Ocean, when a business jet touched down at the International Airport and taxied to the General Aviation Terminal. After the engines were shut down, the co-pilot exited the plane, walked over to the lineman, and spoke with him briefly. He ordered the fuel tanks to be topped off, the galley refreshed, and the refuse tanks emptied.

He then walked to the terminal and entered. After walking up to the counter, he stopped, looked around and finally said, "Hi, I will be in the pilots' lounge while they finish servicing my bird. Where are your restrooms?"

"Down the hall to the right," the sweet, pretty, young girl behind the counter said.

"Thank you," the copilot said and headed down the hall.

A couple of minutes later, a tall, heavy-set, older gentleman walked off the plane, into the terminal, and straight out the front door to a waiting cab.

The copilot finished in the lounge and walked back to the counter. "Sweetie, is my bill ready?" he asked her.

"Yes, sir. She was almost dry, all restocked and ready to fly. Here is your bill," she said smiling as she sat there in her blue shorts and tight white blouse with her name Donna embroidered above her right ample breast.

"Thank you," he said. He pulled out his credit card, paid the bill, took his receipt, and walked out of the terminal toward the plane. He was not aware that his actions had been watched from the moment he stepped off the plane and walked into the terminal. The observer had been sitting in the lounge area reading a newspaper when the plane had landed. When it stopped at the terminal, the observer had stood up and walked behind the counter smiling at Donna and into an office where there were monitors and recording equipment. He watched as the co-pilot entered, stopped

172

at the counter, and then left. But he was more interested in watching the large, heavy-set, older man leave the plane and exit to a waiting car out front. This man had to be his target; he picked up the phone and called his office hoping to catch his partner, Al Lakota.

The pilot was required to file a flight plan with the FAA since their next stop was Los Angeles, California.

"Good morning ladies and gentlemen, I hope you had a restful night because the fun is about to start," Lt. Val Lake of Hawaii Five O said as Connie's team entered the conference room of the Hawaii Five-O' safe house. It was eight o'clock in the morning in sunny Honolulu and everyone looked well rested.

"Not so restful, could not sleep, not even after a good swim," Connie replied, "What do you have?"

"We have a lead. Monahan has been spotted on Kauai. He must feel he is pretty safe over there, but we have informants everywhere," Lake said.

"So what is the plan?" Amber asked not waiting for her mom or Joanne to ask.

"The plan, well, that needs to be decided today and now," Lake said as she looked seriously at the three women and three men sitting across from her. She stood, walked over to the coffee bar, and poured a cup of coffee. "Al should be here in a couple of minutes; traffic at his office slowed him down."

"Okay, we know where he is; let's get him before the Koreans find him and take him out," Josh stated being impatient about getting the man that killed his father and almost killed his mother.

"Trust me, son, we will get him and soon," Lake promised. "War is not a game like your Xbox; and trust me, we are at war with a terrorist named Monahan."

"I know that Miss Lake; when he is dead I will rest better. I want my mom to kill him, not arrest him. Kill him," Josh demanded and then added, "I don't play Xbox or any games."

"I can't let her do that, and you know that. I know the CIA has authority to assassinate when the need is there to protect Americans on foreign soil, but this is not foreign soil. This is the United States. She would go to jail for murder; and you and her team, if assisting, would be charged as accessories."

"We understand that, but accidents happen," Amber slipped in.

"If he turns up dead, well, I will not go into what would happen again. All I will say is that when we attempt to arrest, and if he resists, well, anything can happen. We do have rules of engagement, just like the military; we can't shoot first and then ask questions," Lake added, paused for a second and then continued, "We will move out of here at nine; bring your weapons and wear your vests, just in case. I have a plane waiting for us at the airport to take us to Kauai. We will be met by my team, converge on the compound where Monahan is staying, and then assess the situation before moving in. Understood? Now go, meet back here in thirty minutes. Go!"

"Where the hell is Al?" Lake asked the officer at the front desk when she stepped off the elevator. She received her answer when her friend walked through the door.

"Sorry for being late, heard some disturbing news at the office and wanted to follow up," Al said as he walked over to Val.

"Do you want to discuss it here in the lobby?"

"No, better go upstairs and get your people back in there too," Al said as they walked over to the elevators.

Minutes after getting into the conference room, Al related what his partner had passed on to him.

"When did this happen?" Val asked.

"Yesterday morning, but I just heard the information this morning. My partner left it on my answering machine, because he could not get in touch with me. Sorry for the delay," Al said.

"No problem, we have also received confirmation from other sources that he is on the island. I have ordered everyone to be back here in, well now, in about twenty minutes, we are going to Kauai and do the take down. Are you ready to go?"

"My gear is in the car; it will only take a couple of minutes to grab it."

"Good," Val said.

Chapter 34 North Dakota Gamble

"Brian, we have a problem," Mona Vale said quietly as the two of them sat in front of the big screen television watching the news.

"The only problem we have is that we are almost out of beer," Brian commented with a smile.

"No seriously, Brian. I received a message from the boss. Monahan attempted to kill the Prime Minister of North Korea; he said that war with North Korea is about to happen."

"Okay, what does he want us to do? We are stuck here in North freaking Dakota waiting for what I don't know. War is on the horizon; well, hell, what are we supposed to do? The silos are now apartments, no missiles, nothing bigger than a couple of heavy machine guns and mortars. We can't stop a war," Brian said quietly.

"He doesn't want us to stop the war, but to get this place ready for use; hire doctors and staff," Vale stated.

"Get it ready, sure, right away. Let's watch the end of the news, and then go to work getting things together," Brian said and then turned his attention to the news.

"We have just been informed that the President of the United States will be speaking in a few minutes; please stand by," the news talking head said and then the screen changed to show the briefing room at the White House.

"I guess that goes along with what he told you," Brian commented.

"Good afternoon, America. I have a short announcement, and then I will take questions. Without beating around the bush, I will come right to it. North Korea has declared war with the United States. We are in negotiations with them in an attempt to solve this peacefully. But until that is completed, I am putting all our armed forces on alert. All reservists, please report to your duty stations and await orders. I am meeting with Congress and the Senate in one hour to upgrade our defense forces to the next level. I am not a dictator and cannot respond to this threat without the approval of the government, unless they attack first, which they have not," President Tony Sanford said, "Questions?"

"I have something to show you, Mona. Please come with me," Brian said standing and starting for the door.

"Right behind you babe," Mona said as she followed him out the door. "Where are we going?"

"You will see, just don't say anything until we get there," Brian insisted. As he walked toward the elevators, he pulled a credit card out of his pocket.

Ten minutes later after riding the elevator down to the lowest level, they stepped out and walked to the right toward a door that she had not noticed before. But that was probably because she had not been to this level before.

"Mona, you are my partner and my best two-legged friend; I was on orders to keep this part of the compound secret from everyone, including you. Your clearance level did not go this high until a couple of minutes ago. The President has granted you an interim upgrade in your level," Brian said as he started to unlock the door using the remote key pad and retina scanner.

"How did he do that?" Mona asked confused.

"The exact words the President said in the order he said them was established years ago to tell me remotely what to do and when to do it. Okay, please step inside, and I will brief you on what will happen next," Brian said as they walked in and he closed and locked the door behind them. Standing in a completely dark room with only a few small lights blinking around the room, she felt disoriented. Brian reached over and flipped the light switch to on, casting a low light around the room.

"Holy cow, what the hell is all this?" Mona asked as she looked around the control room. "What does this control? It looks like the bridge to the starship *Enterprise*."

"Please have a seat; and I will explain and train you on how to use it," he said indicating that she should take the chair in the middle of the room.

"The Captain's chair, wow!" she exclaimed.

"In a sense it is, you can control everything with the controls on the arms and watch on the screen in front of you," Brian started.

"What screen?" she interrupted.

"Oops, sorry; this screen," he said as he pressed a button that turned the wall directly in front of her into a large one-hundred-inch color monitor.

"Wow, cool, now it is the starship *Enterprise*. What does it do?"

"This is the control room for a ground based laser system that this site had installed over three years ago. We can't turn it on, but I can show you everything except bringing up the lasers. Four of the silos were not converted to apartments; instead, they have retractable laser guns. Pushing these four buttons will raise the guns to the surface and activate the systems. Your targeting system is across the bottom, numbered one to four. Radar is on the left, there is a powerful tracking antenna system known as the Very Large Array (VLA) located down in New Mexico that provides us with tracking data. If you didn't notice, we are below the lowest level anyone can reach without special knowledge and the key card."

"Is this for real?" Mona asked not believing what she was viewing.

"Yes, it is for real; and we may just have to activate this in defense of our nation. There are four other sites scattered around the country, one each in Oregon, Arizona, Georgia, and Virginia. Mount Weather in northern Virginia is the main headquarters and control center."

"Is this system capable of knocking down an incoming missile?" Mona asked.

"Yes, it has been proven many times on test drones," Brian said; and then added, "The system can come online in less than two minutes. With the power we can generate from the above ground generators and additional transformers located down the hall, we can fire continuously for five hours, longer if we spread out between the four guns and the other sites."

"Does it have the same range and power as the *Enterprise*?" Mona asked as a joke.

"Actually more like the *Death Star* from *Star Wars*," Brian responded.

"Wow, the *Death Star* could destroy whole planets but took twenty to thirty minutes to bring online," Mona commented.

"Yes, but we can be online in two minutes because we store the power and are able to release it on demand. Just like the *Enterprise*."

"One final question, if we are at war, can this place sustain a direct hit from a nuclear bomb?"

"We are over two hundred feet below the surface, below the compound that you know and love," Brian replied, turned and walked over to a door located on the far side of the control room. "Come with me."

"In here is a full suite with kitchen and store room with plenty of food and water," Brian said showing Mona the suite. "There are four suites located in here to house up to four couples or eight singles, plenty of room for you, me, and a few chosen survivors."

"Oh, sounds cool, if we need it."

Chapter 35 Kauai Round Up

The flight over to Kauai was short and uneventful; the sky was a beautiful blue with a few scattered clouds. Landing in Kauai was smooth with a roll out to the end of the runway. The plane turned and taxied to the General Aviation Terminal, and stopped on the far side away from view of the terminal.

Lieutenant Lake and her team along with Connie and her two children and three of her team walked off the plane into the bright sunshine and heat. Al Lakota and his team would arrive on a second plane within minutes.

After grabbing their equipment bags and donning sunglasses, they walked to the waiting vehicles that would take them to the local Hawaii Five O headquarters.

"Good afternoon Lieutenant Lake, welcome to Kauai," the desk sergeant said as they walked into the precinct.

"Afternoon, Henry. How's it hanging?" Lake replied, getting a smile from Henry and then he pointed toward the door on the right.

"They are waiting," Henry said and then added, "Hanging right where your mother left them."

"Dad, good to see you; how's mom?" Lake asked as she walked across the lobby.

"Doing well, you all better get in there. They are steaming," Henry said.

"You're not coming in?" Lake stopped and asked before opening the door.

"No way, being the top cop does give me some privileges and this one is all yours, Val. Now get in there," Henry said and looked at the rest of the team as they came in. "Mrs. Pierce, I am very sorry to hear about Davin; he was a good friend."

"I didn't know you were acquainted," Connie said. "This is Josh and Amber, our children, and this is Charlie Benson and Frank Price."

"Pleasure is all mine; now the boys are waiting for you," Henry said and pointed at the door again.

"Okay, we get the picture, dad," Val said and then opened the door to the room at which his Dad pointed.

"Hello, glad you could make it," the sergeant standing in front said as the team entered. "I understand Lakota will be joining us?"

"Hi Sergeant Glass, is this the team you have assembled for the op? And, yes, Al will be our backup on this op," Lieutenant Lake asked and answered as she entered.

"Yes, is there a problem?" Glass asked.

"No, no, I need to introduce you to my team," Val said and then introduced everyone. After a few minutes of introductions and hand shaking, she walked up to the front of the room and stood beside Sergeant Glass. "You may take a seat or stand here if you want, your choice; but I need to brief everyone from here," she said pushing Glass a little to the side of the podium.

"Oh, yeah, sorry," Glass said stepping to the side and sat in the front row.

"First, do you have anything new on the target?" Val asked Glass.

"Oh, yes, I, ah, we have twenty-four-hour surveillance on the house that Monahan is supposedly staying in and have not seen him since his arrival. We are not completely sure he is even there. The last person we saw going in was an old oriental man with a limp."

"That is probably Monahan in disguise, the limp is where I put a bullet in him in Hong Kong," Connie said.

"Disguise? No way, this guy could barely walk, and did not fit the description you provided us. This guy is so old he could barely get out of the cab. He carried no luggage, just a small backpack," Glass commented, "Here, we have a picture of him," he said pulling a photo out of the folder on the desk.

"That has to be him, right height and build. It has to be him," Connie replied after looking at the photo. "But we need a way to make sure. If we bust in, and he is the wrong guy; well, the law suits would roll in faster than your patrol cars."

"She's right; we need a way to make sure. Any suggestions?" Val asked the team.

"Yeah," Josh spoke up.

"What's the plan, Josh?" Val asked.

"Simple we just knock on the door and see who answers," Josh said simply.

"Yeah, simple, but he has seen all of you and probably would recognize a cop from a mile away," Val said.

"That may not work," Glass said.

"Why not?" Josh asked.

"The property is private; you have to get in the gate which is where the door bell is. Once in, you have a quarter mile to drive before getting to the house. They have security systems in place, as well as guards; this place is a fortress. Without an invitation, you can't get in. It used to belong to George Harrison of Beatles fame and he loved his privacy. When he died, the estate was sold to a corporation which uses it for parties and special guests. I guess Monahan qualifies as a special guest."

"Is it possible that the corporation is owned by Rocky Soto?" Joanne asked.

"We don't know for sure, but possible," Glass added.

"Shit. Okay Plan B," Josh said.

"Watch your language Josh, please," Connie scolded.

"Sorry, mom. But Plan B," Josh said.

"What is Plan B?" Val asked looking at Davin's only son.

"Plan B is to go in covertly, like James Bond would do. Sneak in and plant some bugs or cameras or just look in the windows," Josh replied.

"Sounds great, except we are the police, not spies. And you guys cannot legally do it either on U.S. soil. So what is your next great plan?" Val said and then looked around the room, "Any other ideas?"

"I like Josh's idea," Connie said. "Charlie is a trained field agent and can get in and out without being seen."

"I can't approve that," Val stated.

"What about water access?" Amber asked.

"Yes, there is a beach on the property; and the right person could get on shore that way. Maybe we drive a boat past taking pictures," Glass said and then added, "Oh, we have already done that. The pictures are in the folder in front of you, L.T. They don't show anyone except the old man, a young woman, and two younger men. She, being the maid, who leaves at five every day, and the two men are bodyguards, we believe."

"You observed all this in one day of watching?" Val asked.

"Yes, been a slow week on the island," Glass responded and then added, "Your dad wanted us out of the building and doing something besides taking up space in here."

"Sounds like him," Val agreed. "Okay, so I guess for lack of a better plan we just knock on the door and see what happens. I will do the knocking. The rest of you will back me up."

"What's the reason to knock?" Connie asked.

"Simple, my car will break down in front of his gate. I will be wearing very short shorts and a bikini top, to distract the guards a bit."

"Yeah, it would distract me," Glass commented before Josh had a chance to say the same thing, getting nods from all the men in the room.

"Knock it off; at four this afternoon, I will break down at the gate. Can you fix me up with a mini camera or something to get some pictures," Val asked.

"Sure we can fix you up with a mini cam. How small is your bikini top?" Connie asked.

"Small, but big enough to cover these," Val said pointing to her fairly large breasts. "But barely."

"No problem," Connie replied.

Three hours later, Lieutenant Lake was driving back from the beach near the property where Monahan was supposedly staying. She was dressed in a very tiny bikini top, showing a lot of skin, and short cutoff jeans bottom, which barely covered more than her bikini. As she approached the gate, her car started to spit and sputter right on cue, stalling just past the gate. She pulled over and rolled to a stop, shook her head, and slammed her hand on the steering wheel. After saying some choice words to the car that it would not understand anyway, she attempted to start the car without any luck.

She opened the door, slid out, walked around the front, and opened the hood, leaning over to look inside as if that would help start it. Not more than two minutes after stopping, the gate swung open and a man in plaid shorts and Hawaiian shirt walked out and over to her.

"What's the problem, Miss?" the man asked.

"I don't know; it just quit," Val replied. "Do you know anything about cars?"

"Sure, let me take a look," he said and then leaned in and looked over the engine. Seeing no obvious problem, he walked around to the door and sat inside. He turned the key, and attempted to start it. He then looked at the gas gauge and stated, "Miss, I think I found the problem. You are out of gas."

"What, I just filled it up this morning before going to the beach," Val yelled and walked around to the door and leaned in, giving the man a close up view of her breasts.

"Yes, you are out of fuel. Let me out; I would like to check and see if you have a leak somewhere," he said turning to look her in the eye, trying his best not to be overly observant of her nearly naked body so close to his.

After getting out, he went back to look at the engine examining the fuel line and connections, and could not find a leak. Then he pulled out the floor mat from the front and kneeled down to look at the fuel tank, using the mat as a cushion for his knees. He saw no leaks there either. Finally, he went to the gas cap and found it missing.

"Looks like someone stole your gas cap and took your gas too, while you were on the beach," he said. "Look, I may have some gas in the garage; would you care to come with me to get it or wait here?" he offered.

"If you don't mind, I will follow you; and if possible, do you have a bathroom I could use? Drank too much Gator Aid today," she asked.

"I think we can help in both areas. You may want to lock your car first. We don't have much crime out here, but you can never be too careful," he said. After she locked the car, they started for the gate, he punched in a code and the gate slowly opened.

They walked over to a golf cart parked beside the row of bushes and climbed in.

"Wow, how far is it to the garage?" she asked innocently.

"Not too far, can walk it in about twenty minutes, but the property is pretty big and it is much easier to get around in the cart. Property is about eight acres with about a thousand feet of beach, the owner likes his privacy and this place gives it," he explained as he drove.

"Must be worth a fortune, compared to my little apartment. What do you do here?"

"I take care of the grounds; you know, mow the grass, trim the bushes, general upkeep," he responded.

"Who owns this place?" she asked.

"You know I can't tell you that; remember, he likes his privacy and that is part of my job, keeping him private. So enough questions from you. What do you do that gives you the day off to enjoy the beach?"

"Not much, I am a spoiled rich kid gone bad; spending all of daddy's money and only working when I have to," she teased. "No, really, I am a customer service technical service rep and work the evening shift for Microsoft, which allows me to work from home and play during the day," Val said as she told him her cover story.

"Interesting, you must get a lot of calls."

"Not as many as they used to get a few years ago before I started. They tell me stories that a single tech would get upwards of fifty to a hundred plus calls per shift. Most could be handled quickly, but others took a while. It must have been insane."

"I don't think I could handle the calls," he said and stopped in front of the garage, "Wait here. No, don't wait, come with me; there is a bathroom inside the beach house behind the garage. Go through that door and up the stairs." He waited at the foot of the stairs until she returned and then they both walked back to the cart. He placed a full five-gallon gas can in the back of the cart and they started back to the gate.

Twenty-five minutes later, he had poured the fuel in the tank and had the car started.

"Thank you, ah. You know I never heard your name," Val said as she looked up at him from the front seat of her now running car.

"Sorry, Bruce. My name is Bruce. You have a safe day and get a locking gas cap," Bruce said and then walked back to the gate and watched her drive off, smiling.

She was smiling too. While he was getting the gas, she had been able to place several small cameras around the outside of the garage and one just inside the door. She reached over to the center console, pulled out her cell phone, and pressed speed dial three.

"Are you receiving a signal?" Val asked.

"Yes, perfect. Thanks, come on back to the station," Glass said and then hung up.

Forty minutes later, after stopping at her hotel to change, she walked into the precinct and sat beside Glass to view the monitors showing the property she just left.

Chapter 36 Target Rich Environment

"Sir, we have incoming!" the radar operator yelled.

"Stats?" the senior man on duty yelled back.

"Four, not yet reached Apex, projected targets are, wait, Seattle, LA, Denver, and San Francisco," the operator replied quickly after doing some very quick range and impact points.

"Hell!" the senior op exclaimed and picked up the red phone and waited for an answer, which was only seconds, but seemed like hours.

"Sir, we have four inbound bogies; projected impact in forty-five minutes, LA, Seattle, Denver, and San Fran." He reported that World War Three just started with a nuclear strike from North Korea; and after pausing for a second, added, "This is an exercise; repeat, this is an exercise."

"Thank you, stand by," was the response received, and then the line went dead.

In the war room under the White House, President Tony Sanford and his advisors sat and listened to the report. Sanford stood and walked over to the coffee pot and poured himself a cup, looked at the rest of the room, and pointed to the pot indicating he would pour if anyone wanted a cup. He received one response from Hallie Norge, his personal secretary.

"Okay lady and gentlemen, if this were a real alert, what do we do?" Sanford asked the room.

"Now..." he was interrupted when the phone rang again.

Hallie Norge picked up the phone and said, "War room."

"This is not an exercise notification. May I speak to the President," the voice said quietly.

"Just a moment, please," Hallie said, covered the mouth piece, and told the President, "Call for you sir."

"Hello, this is President Sanford," he said when he took the handset; he listened for a moment and hung up without saying another word.

"We have another problem," Sanford said and then sat down at the head of the table, picked up his coffee cup, and sipped carefully.

"What could be worse than a nuclear war with Korea and China?" one of the advisors asked.

"Biological warfare. One of our operatives in North Korea has uncovered information that both North Korea and China have developed and are capable of launching both nuclear and biological weapons on their ICBMs. And worse yet, they are unsure of the type of bio weapon that is being loaded on the missiles. Which means, we don't know how to counteract the bio weapon."

"If the wind shifts, it could blow the nuclear fallout or biological all across the country, no stopping it," General Whitmore commented. "We need to stop the launch of those missiles or at least destroy them before re-entry."

"I have to agree with you General; but we can't launch to destroy their launch sites until they launch first. Otherwise, we will be starting the war. I want to continue negotiations with hopes to prevent war all together," Sanford said. "I will not be the President that starts the war; I am the President that ends the war, or prevents one."

"What do we do, sir? If we wait, and they launch, and Star Wars misses or fails, and they reach apex and re-enter the atmosphere? We will be toast, literally," Hallie asked, knowing she had no right to speak during the meeting. "Sorry, sir."

"That's alright, Hallie; this concerns you just as much as the rest of us. But again, I will not start the war; I will warn them that if we get indication that they are or have launched, we will eliminate their country as quickly as we can. There will be no survivors in North Korea, none. Total destruction. They know we can, and are betting we will not do it. But trust me, we will do it." After pausing for a moment, he looked at Hallie and said, "Hallie, get the Prime Minister of North Korea on the secure line. If he will not talk to me then get his highest advisor."

"Yes, sir," Hallie said. She walked back over to the table with the phones, picked up the handset for the blue phone, and spoke into the handset.

"Mr. Prime Minister, this is President Sanford of the United States of America, we need to talk and resolve this before it gets out of hand," Sanford said to the PM.

"Sir, I respect your call, but there is nothing to be done except the destruction of your country. Your country attacked me and almost killed me while I was conducting business peacefully," the PM's translator said and then paused to listen to the PM again.

"We are prepared to fight to the death, is your country?" the translator said.

"Sir, with all due respect, I am calling you to find a way around the destruction of either country. Many lives will be lost on both sides, and the world may lose more from the fallout. Do you want that? I don't think you do, because a good leader wants only to see his country prosper. We fought once ending with a divided country; if you ever want to get Korea back together, you need to stand down."

"No, Mr. President, we are going to launch; and you can do whatever you need to do. But you attacked my country first, and I will finish this war with your death."

"Mr. Prime Minister, I understand what you are saying; but you can be sure that before your first missile strikes my country, I will rain every nuclear missile I have in my arsenal on your country and China if I have to. The destruction of your countries will be total, no survivors. And you are already aware that we have tactical nuclear missiles in South Korea aimed at your capital and will launch at the first sign of your missiles leaving their silos. Do you understand Mr. Prime Minister, total destruction, no survivors? Are you prepared to die?"

"I will let you know in one hour, my decision, Mr. President," the translator said and then broke the connection.

"Do you think he will back down?" Hallie asked.

"No, he is stubborn and I believe a bit stupid," Sanford said and then added, "Raise to DEFCON One, Nuclear War Imminent!"

"Yes, sir," General Whitmore said. He picked up the secure phone, and placed the order to his command post.

"Anyway you look at it, whether we are the target or North Korea is the target, to quote a phrase from the movie *'Top Gun'* it is ah, or rather one of our countries will be a *'Target Rich Environment.'*" Sanford commented casually, but not smiling.

"Lock and load," Whitmore added with a smile.

Chapter 37 Rocky and Horatio

Rocky Soto was flying to Bombay, India. He was to arrive late in the afternoon, the day after the attack on him and the Prime Minister in Hong Kong. After being treated by the medics for gunshot wounds and advised by the police not to leave the country, he slipped out of his room and made his way to the airport, boarded his private jet and flew to Bombay.

"Hello," Rocky said into his cell phone during the flight; he was surprised to hear his son's voice.

"Hello father, where are you?" Horatio asked.

"On my way to Bombay, where are you?"

"Up in the air right now, but I will be in Bombay soon. Are you going to the Penthouse?" Horatio said.

"Yes, when will you be here?"

"Two days at least," Horatio said on the inflight telephone. "I have to stop in L.A. to pick up a package before I fly over."

"Good, yes, I will be at the penthouse. See you in two days," Rocky said, and then broke the connection. He sat wondering what his son was up to.

"Captain, when do we land?" Rocky asked his pilot as he stepped through the door to the cockpit.

"We should be on the ground in a couple of hours," the pilot commented after looking over at the DME and checking the inflight GPS.

"Good, call ahead for a car and driver. And get the plane serviced, we may need to leave quickly," Rocky ordered.

"Yes, sir," the pilot replied and then returned his attention to flying the jet. Rocky returned to his seat and contemplated his next move. He had succeeded in his talks with the Prime Minister of North Korea and now hoped that side of the plan would work. He sat there thinking about the attack on the Prime Minister and came to the conclusion that his son may have been behind the attack.

192

Only one person knew about the meeting, Horatio. Of course, the Prime Minister and his people knew, but why would he want to have someone attack and almost kill him. So, Horatio was obviously the one behind the attack. He would have to speak to him and find out what was going on.

Horatio sat quietly in the back of his jet and thought about his father. His father was a genius, but lacked common sense. The attack had been put together by Horatio per the request of the Prime Minister. He wasn't told the reason, but figured North Korea needed an excuse to start a war and having the attack done by American CIA agents was the perfect way to start a war. The PM had even told Horatio to have Rocky Soto killed during the attack; that would solidify the CIA attack as well as the fact that another American was there for reasons unknown to anyone other than the Prime Minister.

"Kelly, time to go. Let's get this bird off the ground," Horatio ordered his pilot.

"Destination, sir?" the pilot replied as he looked at the chart of Los Angeles International Airport that was on his lap.

"Honolulu then on to Bombay, India." Horatio replied.

"We can leave in about two hours, sir. Need to refuel and restock the food for that long of a trip. Is two hours okay?" the pilot questioned.

"Yes, and then to Seoul, Korea. Any problem with that?"

"As you wish, it will take a few minutes to put together the flight plan," the pilot responded.

"OK, add the fuel," Horatio replied a little pissed that they couldn't leave immediately.

"Yes, plenty, but you said North Dakota when you called; we have more than enough for that, but not enough for Hawaii, then Bombay; it won't take long, the truck is already pulling up. And I need to file a flight plan," the pilot said seeing the fuel truck stop near the fuel port.

"Can't you do that in the air?" Horatio asked, and then thought, what the hell, a few more minutes on the ground in L.A. would not change the outcome of his plan. He had picked up his package; and it was safely strapped into the seat in the back. His men had made true their promise and there she was. She came willingly because they had threatened to kill multiple people including her father and everyone in the company she worked for if she didn't cooperate. To prove they were serious, they had shot and killed two of her Secret Service agents.

"No, sir, since North Korea declared war, the FAA and all countries are on alert. If we don't have a valid flight plan on file, we could get shot down before entering Korean airspace. Even with the flight plan on file, we still are at risk. Do you still want to stop in Seoul?"

"Yes, I need about an hour on the ground to tie up some loose ends."

Two hours later, they lifted off the ground, departed Los Angeles airspace, and headed toward Honolulu.

Chapter 38 If I Only Had A Brain

"Follow the yellow brick road, my dear. Just follow the yellow brick road," Brian said to Mona as they left the underground control center. She looked down and saw a faded yellow strip on the concrete leading from the elevator to the door they had just exited.

"Wow, who would have thought?" Mona said when they reached the elevator. "Makes me remember the other catch phrase from the Wizard of Oz."

"What's that?" Brian asked as he pushed the up button for the elevator.

"If I only had a Brian. Get it, Brian," she said laughing.

"You mean brain, don't you; you already have a Brian," he added.

"Oh, you old stick in the mud. Just like Rodney Dangerfield, mixing up the words, Brian for Brain. Get it?" Mona tried to explain.

"Yes, honey I get it, who's old? Now, when we get upstairs, do not mention anything about what I showed you down here. And use only this elevator to access it. I have disconnected the camera and microphones in this one; and it is the only one that will go below level seven," Brian said as he stepped into the elevator.

"Right, baby, got you covered," Mona said and then followed him into the elevator. "What's our next move?"

"Our next move is to monitor the news, and wait until either Monahan shows up or is killed. You need to keep your phone close to you at all times; in case I am unavailable, you will need to go down and activate the system. We may be going to war very soon and I want to be completely ready if that happens. Let's hope the President can calm the North Koreans down."

"I hope he can," Mona agreed.

"Mr. President, Mr. Kline is on the phone, do you want to take the call?" Hallie asked him through the open door of the Oval Office.

"Yes, put him through," Tony Sanford said and then after the first ring, he picked up the handset and said, "Good afternoon, what can the office of the President do for the head of NSA?"

"It is not what your office can do for us, but what we can do for you," Walter Kline, Director of NSA said.

"Okay, please go on."

"I told you I would keep you up to date on any intelligence we get out of North Korea and I really need to come over and brief you on the latest developments. I know this line is secure, but you need to see the evidence we have collected instead of just hearing it. When can I come over?"

"How about now; I will clear my calendar. Do we need anyone else in this impromptu meeting?" Sanford asked.

"Yes, the usual suspects would be good. I will be there in an hour; can we get the team together by then?" Kline asked.

"By order of my office, they will be here or be looking for new jobs," Sanford commented smiling. Kline knew he really didn't mean it, but also knew he had the power to do it if need be.

"One hour, I will alert the kitchen to be ready if we run late," Sanford said and then laid the handset back in its cradle. He leaned back in his chair, closed his eyes, and attempted to drop into deep thought.

A lot was going on in the world; and if Korea decided to act on their threat, it could bring the end to life on this planet as we have grown to know it. The use of nuclear or biological weapons would lay waste to more than half of the civilized world. Bringing to bare a lot of what Hollywood has put into movies about waste lands, cannibals, walking dead and the horrors of the type of destruction that was possible, all created by man. What man has created, man can destroy.

At precisely one hour after the phone call and the ordering of the usual suspects, Hallie tapped on the Oval Office door. She stuck her head in, and announced, "Sir, your visitors are here."

"Show them in and hold all calls until we are done. Unless it is the PM of North Korea of course," Sanford ordered. Once everyone was in, the door closed, and all seated comfortably around the coffee table, he asked, "Does anyone need a drink, coffee, water?"

"Director Kline, since everyone passed on drinks for now, what information do you have for us?" Sanford asked after getting no reply on the drink request.

"Sirs and Ladies, the situation has become even more deadly in the past couple of hours. Our sources have uncovered indicators that ISIS is planning a coordinated attack from within the boundaries of our borders. The exact location is unknown, but we are working on it; should have details shortly. Additionally, we have intercepted communications between ISIS and North Korea concerning the purchase of nuclear weapons of mass destruction," Kline reported, pausing for a moment to let it sink in.

"Wow, that isn't good. Okay, we are the decision makers in this; and I need your input and suggestions. But before we get deep into that, I have good news to add. I have received positive confirmation that China is stepping down from any potential hostilities, saying it would not be good for business. The business relationship they have established between us would hurt their economy more if the war broke out. They do not want to commit economic suicide by war as it were. Looks like they decided to use their brain to protect their country and not follow a mad man into a war that would destroy too much," President Sanford said and then looked intently at his team, "We have some serious decisions to make about Korea and ISIS and need to do it now."

"Sir, we can't fight a war on two fronts; we don't have enough troops, weapons and material," General Whitmore stated.

"That we know, but we knew that at the start of World War II and the country came together and we built what we needed and won a war on two fronts. We did it then, and we can do it again. We have the technology and resources to do it. We have to do it again, or die trying," Sanford stated.

"This is all true, but it wasn't until the end of World War II when we dropped a couple of Atomic Bombs, ending the war with Japan and had planned on using one on Berlin but never did, for several reasons," Whitmore said. After pausing he continued, "This war will start and end in a matter of hours or days, because it will start with weapons of mass destruction. Who is to say how long we, or they, will last, days maybe; but in my educated opinion this war will end in less than a week, tops. And what it will leave is millions dead or dying. Destruction of major cities and infrastructure, mass hunger, government either in shambles or completely destroyed. Should I go on."

"No, we get the picture and I believe Hollywood has done several disaster movies based on exactly that," Sanford said, not smiling.

A knock on the door interrupted the meeting. Sanford stood and with a lot of anger in his eyes opened the door to be greeted by the Director of the FBI.

"What, I am in a private meeting," Sanford said a little too loud.

"Sir, I know you are in a meeting but this is extremely important, can we talk for a moment, privately," the director asked.

"What can me more important than trying to prevent a war?"

"Your daughter, sir. She has been kidnapped," the director said quietly, hoping nobody else would hear.

"What?" Sanford asked and then pulled the director down the hall a short way and stared into his eyes. "What did you say?"

"Your daughter has been kidnapped."

At six o'clock Hawaii time, a private business jet touched down and rolled to a stop in front of the General Aviation terminal of Kauai International Airport. Four passengers walked down the air stair to a waiting gray Chevy SUV. Throwing their bags in the back, each climbed in and the driver drove off the airport and into the traffic. Forty minutes later, the driver stopped in front of the Kauai Hilton Hotel and Suites.

Sue Lynn, Victoria and two specially trained Korean Secret Service Field Operatives climbed out of the vehicle; and after gathering their bags, entered the hotel and checked in. Their rooms had already been reserved and paid for in advance.

Their arrival at the airport and hotel did not go unnoticed. Director Kline had ordered all of his field operatives to be on the lookout for Sue Lynn and Victoria. They were monitoring all flights in and out of Hawaii and every international airport in CONUS. There was no way those two could enter the country without being seen. The report went back up to NSA and CIA within minutes after being spotted. And now, they were being watched by both NSA and CIA agents.

A late-night flight from Iran brought three ISIS members to a meeting with two North Korean representatives in Bombay, India. The discussion was about weapons of mass destruction.

The airport was under the watchful eye of our close allies from Israel, the Mossad. Many said the Mossad were as good as the U.S. Intelligence community, but others would dispute that by saying they were better. No matter whom you believed, the Mossad were damn good at what they did. They spotted the three ISIS members the second they stepped off the private plane; and when the Koreans arrived, they were also closely watched.

The agents of Mossad reported their findings to their headquarters which in turn sent a message to both the NSA and CIA local stations, who transmitted the find to HQ. Within thirty minutes, the information was on Josh Randal's desk.

"Holy crap," Josh said to himself. He pressed the intercom button and asked Meredith to come in and bring a fresh bottle of scotch.

Chapter 39 Finger On the Trigger

"It is eight in the morning and we are almost all here. Where is Charlie?" Lieutenant Vale asked the team when they assembled in the conference room.

"Charlie will be down in a minute. He called me and said he had eaten something that did not agree with his stomach. As soon..." Connie reported and was cut off by Vale.

"We have the picture. Did he go to the Sushi Bar on the corner? Its ratings are in the bucket; and they have had a lot of violations recently," Vale cut in, and then asked, "Did anyone else eat there?"

Getting a no from everyone else satisfied her question that they either did not eat there or had strong stomachs. "The rest of you either didn't eat there, or are just very lucky. We need to move on." After pausing for a second to take a sip of her coffee, she continued, "We now have confirmation that Monahan is on the estate. The cameras I planted yesterday took a good shot of him stepping out on the back patio without his disguise. I think we need to act fast or he will be gone. Glass, have you heard anything new from your contacts?" Vale asked.

"Yes, not sure if it applies, but I don't believe in coincidences. There was a flight plan filed by a business jet, departing North Korean airspace that is now heading for Kauai. Estimated arrival is at nine this morning. The flight plan was originally filed through Seoul and modified by the pilot in flight to land in Kauai. That is normal procedure for aircraft departing from Communist countries."

"Interesting, are they sending a jet to move him or bringing reinforcements?" Joanne asked.

"Could be either, the passenger lists indicated seven on board not including the pilot, copilot and crew," Glass said.

"I would expect it is for reinforcements for Sue Lynn's team," Connie added, "Why would North Korea send a plane to move him; that would come out of Hong Kong or the States."

"Are there any unscheduled flights coming from the States?" Amber asked.

"There are at least a dozen from the States arriving daily to Honolulu, Kauai, and Maui. They bring everyone from rock stars to golfers looking to beat our courses. That is not counting the charter flights that bring in hundreds daily, full of tourists and anyone that can't afford or don't want to wait for a scheduled flight. Remember the islands are an extremely popular tourist destination. We cannot monitor every flight, even though we try," Glass responded.

"It was a just a thought, but what if more of Monahan's men show up and reinforce him? Mom did say he had sixty or eighty men in his militia. Would he bring them here, or run for the hills of North Dakota?" Amber queried looking for an answer.

"That is the million-dollar question. But, right now, we know where he is, and we need to get him now," Connie stated.

"Agreed," Vale said, "And this is how we are going to do it."

Twenty minutes later, she had outlined a plan that hopefully would bring Monahan to justice or to a quick grave.

"We move out in one hour; now get your gear and make sure you bring all your noise, big and small," Val ordered just as Charlie walked in looking like he had just spent the past hour draining his stomach from both ends.

"Sorry for being late. Did I miss anything?" Charlie asked.

"Yes, and no. You are in no condition to go on this op, so get yourself some stomach medicine from the pharmacy downstairs and go back to bed," Connie ordered.

"Connie, I am fine; I will never eat Sushi again," Charlie replied, but not with much feeling.

"No, give your extra ammo to Josh and Amber. I want them armed and dangerous," Connie ordered. She looked at her twins, smiled, and said, "I cannot stop you from going, but I can surely make sure you are armed. I know you can protect yourself. So, go with Charlie, get his extra, and make sure you have your vests on and weapons loaded."

"Okay, mom," Josh and Amber said in unison.

"Okay, mom," Charlie said not sounding very happy, but understanding he would be a liability being sick. "Come on kids, let's go; I have a few toys that will make you very happy."

A few minutes later, the room was empty except for Connie, Val and Joanne.

"What is it?" Val asked looking at the two women.

"Your plan sounds great, coming in from the water and the other three sides at the same time, but he is armed and extremely dangerous. He will not go easy and there may be some, well, let's just say, a firefight where people could get killed. Are you and your cops prepared for that?"

"Ladies, it is what we do; and you need to get ready. We leave in fifty minutes. And I have to order some boats and helicopter for backup," Val said picking up the phone on the desk.

"We will be ready," Connie said and they left the room.

The drive to Waimea would take about an hour and then another ten minutes to get to the estate on the south side of the island. It would be another ten minutes to get into position. The whole operation should not take more than fifteen minutes once kicked off.

The helicopter was in the air and southeast of the estate at five hundred feet over the beach. Two teams in boats were cruising off shore until given the signal to move in; and there were two teams on each side of the estate. Everything was ready to move. Everyone, just needed the go from Val. All were on edge, but confident they would succeed.

"Check in, when in position," Val ordered. She looked over at Al Lakota and received the nod to go on her command. His team had taken up the outer perimeter in case Monahan was able to slip through her team.

"Air, check."

"Team One, check." Each team checked in ready as ordered.

The next command would put her team and the members of the CIA in harm's way once again. The team she had consisted of trained SWAT members and CIA agents, except for two, Josh and Amber Pierce. They had training from their mother and father. They knew what to do and were ready to pull the trigger if need be.

"Go, go!" Val yelled into the radio and then she had her driver run her SWAT truck through the gate and race down the long driveway as the other teams climbed or vaulted over the walls. She was accompanied by Connie, her twins, and a driver. They did not get very far before the windshield and side of the truck were hit by multiple bullets.

The two boats raced toward the beach and ran up onto the beach. Two agents jumped out of each and headed for the house; one agent stayed with each of the boats. Teams raced toward the house from each side, taking cover when they started to receive fire from unseen guards.

Two agents fell before reaching the grass; they were only forty feet from the water's edge. The others dropped behind a low seawall. The SWAT truck continued down the driveway where it was hit more than a hundred times. Since it did not slow down, the shooter decided to try shooting the tires, not knowing they were run flats. Obviously, that effort did not stop the armored vehicle.

The helicopter was hovering over the beach watching for anyone trying to make an escape on a boat, but had to back off when several bullets slammed into the side of the bird. The pilot immediately pulled up and back to keep from taking any more hits.

Bullets were flying all over from both sides. Suddenly, a Humvee burst through the garage doors and raced toward the gate. Shots were fired, but the vehicle was able to get past the SWAT vehicle and raced to the gate. Connie and Val jumped out of their vehicle and fired on the Humvee. Unexpectedly, the Humvee stopped, the passenger door swung open, and out stepped Monahan with an M-4 modified automatic weapon. He immediately opened fire on the two women.

Connie went down instantly as three bullets slammed into her. Val dove for cover evading being hit, and continued to fire on Monahan. He stopped shooting, and jumped back into the Humvee. Josh and Amber jumped out and started to pour lead into the Humvee, hitting the tail lights and blowing out the back window. They did not know if they hit Monahan as the vehicle sped out the gate. Two patrol cars were blocking the gate. The Humvee slammed into the one on the right and sped past. The other took up pursuit, but was stopped when a hand grenade flew out of the Humvee and exploded under the car, killing both officers immediately.

Monahan chuckled at his escape and then grimaced in pain from the two bullets he took in his shoulder. He looked down at his shirt; all he could see was blood everywhere.

"Air Two, follow that Humvee!" Val yelled into her radio and then looked over at the kids.

"Damn, are you kids okay?" Val asked and then looked over at Connie.

"Yes, but mom isn't," Amber yelled.

"Crap!" is all she said when she saw Connie lying in a pool of blood and not moving. Josh and Amber ran over to their mother, dropping their weapons as they reached her. She was alive, but barely.

"Air One, land, we have wounded!" Val ordered the first helicopter to return and pick up the wounded. Within ten minutes, Connie was aboard Air One in flight to the closest hospital with Josh and Amber beside her. The two wounded agents sat in the back with minor wounds still needing medical attention.

When they were gone, Val checked with the rest of the team and found that she had four dead officers. Two were from the boat entry effort, and the other two were in the patrol car that exploded outside the gate. The guards on the estate did not fare very well; four were dead, two wounded and five arrested. Two escaped, including Monahan. The intel Val had was that there were only four guards, but it turned out to be twelve heavily armed mercenaries in addition to Monahan. One of the dead was the guard that helped Val with her 'out of gas' car two days ago. The bad part was that Monahan and one other escaped capture. They were in the wind, and she had only one chance to catch them.

"Dad, Monahan got away. Send a team to the airport; maybe he will head over there. I have Air Two in pursuit; but with the heavy tree cover, they are not having a lot of luck locating them," Val asked her father the chief of police on Kauai.

"Right away, come on back to H.Q," Henry said. "Did you lose any?"

"Yes, dad, we lost a few; and Connie and two others are on the way to the hospital. I will be in after a stop at the hospital. I will give you a complete report when I get back," Val agreed; and then after a complete search of the estate, she and her team left, leaving a couple of officers to guard the place until the Forensic team arrived and took over.

Chapter 40 Tropical Sunset

Josh and Amber Pierce were in the waiting room. Josh was wearing a hole in the carpet as he paced back and forth across the room.

"Josh, please sit down; your pacing is driving me insane," Amber ordered as she sat calmly in the uncomfortable chair in the corner.

"Amber, my little sister, our mother is in surgery, and may not make it out; and you sit there quietly as if nothing has happened," Josh almost yelled but restrained himself a bit.

"Any word?" Val Lake asked as she walked into the waiting room, still wearing her police tactical uniform. She saw both kids waiting for word about their mother also wearing their issued tactical uniforms minus weapons.

"No, been in surgery ever since we arrived. Nurse came out a bit ago and ran down the hall. Not sure why, or where she went, but ran back into the operating room minutes later. She did not say anything, but we could see she was covered in blood," Amber commented with no emotion in her voice, as if she was in another world. She was mentally elsewhere; she could not believe what had happened and what could happen next. But she was the calm member of the family, and her brain just never slept. Mentally, she was making a plan to kill Monahan for the death of her father and shooting of her mother. When the plan formed, she would take Josh aside, explain what they would do, and how. There would be only one of two outcomes of her plan; either Monahan would be dead, or they would.

"Look, kids, she is strong and will get through this. Besides, she needs to hunt down and kill Monahan. I know she will do that," Val said, but not smiling.

"Lieutenant Lake, we are sure she will get through this, but we can't wait until she is up and running again. Josh and I will continue with the hunt and take down of Monahan. Whatever it takes, we can handle it. Both of us are trained and ready. Since we are not officially with the company, that makes us the most logical choice. We can operate in the mainland and work closely with the FBI and local police to make it happen. And if Monahan accidently gets shot and dies during the arrest, he is obviously genetically inferior; and, well, inferior people should not be breathing our air and occupying our land," Amber said confidently and without emotion. She was confident they would succeed or die trying.

"My team is still looking for him. They found the Humvee in which he escaped abandoned four miles from the estate. There was blood on the seat, and a lot of holes, but no Monahan. We are checking the airport and marinas for him, but so far no luck. This guy is good and right now is a ghost," Val stated.

"What is your gut feeling, Lieutenant?" Josh asked.

"I don't think he will try the airport, too many cameras; and we would pick him up as soon as he stepped out of his vehicle. He has two options, boat or helicopter. There are a lot of both on the island. He could charter either option to move to another island and then fly or just hide out. The islands are small, but there are many ways to arrive and leave and even more to hide," Val said.

"Damn!" Amber exclaimed. She immediately stood and stormed out of the waiting room almost running down a doctor about to enter the room. "Oh, sorry!"

"That's okay, young lady; are you the daughter of Mrs. Pierce?" the doctor said quietly.

"Yes, and this is my brother Josh, and Lieutenant Lake of Hawaii Five-O," Amber replied as she wiped the tears from her puffy eyes.

"Good, please if you will take a seat. I need to talk with both of you. Lieutenant, you may stay if you like," the doctor stated and indicated the chairs against the wall.

"Is our mom, all right?" Josh asked quickly.

"Please have a seat. Your mom is resting and should fully recover, but it will take a while. She was hit with three nine-millimeter halo-point bullets. All were the armor piercing variety, two in her side and one in her chest, which penetrated her vest. The ones in the right side damaged her kidney, and the one in the chest grazed her heart. We were able to stop the bleeding and hopefully save her kidney, but only time will tell on that one. We will monitor her and take appropriate action when needed. That is only part of the problem. The damage to her heart was much worse. We temporarily repaired the damage and she is on a heart pump right now and will be for a while. We are hoping the heart will mend itself. I have put an order in for a new heart, hoping one is available and healthy. If so, we will do a heart transplant which with today's technology will bring her back to almost a hundred percent. The other option is to use an artificial heart; there have been great advances in technology and 3D printing that have resulted in the creation of living organs for several years now. The heart is particularly tricky, but there are over a thousand people now living with an artificial heart and doing quite well. If we can't find a healthy heart, that is an alternate option. You need to discuss it with your mom when she wakes up and decide. We may not have much time if hers fails," the doctor stated coldly.

"But she is alive?" Amber questioned.

"She is lucky to be alive at all. Mentally and physically she is alive and breathing, but we will most likely have to do a heart transplant in a few weeks. We have to wait until she is stronger before doing any more surgery," the doctor concluded.

"What can we do to help?" Josh asked looking at his sister, Val, and then back to the doctor.

"Get some rest; she will need support when she wakes up."

"When do you think that will be?" Amber questioned.

"Can't say for sure; we have her in an induced coma to ease the pain and be able to administer the proper drugs to help her recover," the doctor answered. He did not get a very satisfied look from anyone in the room.

"Thank you, doctor. When can we see her?" Josh said. He stood, walked to the door, and opened it for the doctor as he exited.

"She is in recovery and then down to ICU. Not for a couple of days at least, we want to limit contact to prevent any infection. I hope you understand," the doctor said just outside the door and then walked down the hall toward the operating room.

"Val, we need to go after Monahan, when can we get a ride to our hotel. I think I know where he is heading," Amber stated.

"Where might that be, Amber?" Val asked as she stood and walked to the door behind Amber and Josh.

"Mom told me about the compound in North Dakota. He has friends and weapons there. I believe he is heading back home to get reinforcements and weapons. I want to be there to greet him," Amber stated without a smile and no emotion in her voice, except for a lot of anger.

"My car is out front, let's go," Val said leading them toward the parking lot.

Chapter 41 Convergence

Eighteen and a half hours later, Josh, Amber, Joanne, and Charlie stepped off the company business jet in Bismarck, North Dakota. They had left two agents in Hawaii to work with Val and also to monitor Connie's condition. The weather was cool and crisp with a light scattering of snow on the ground. Winter was coming early in North Dakota.

"Damn, I should have packed a heavier jacket," Joanne said as they walked toward the General Aviation terminal.

"At least mom doesn't have to worry about the cold; and I am grateful Val was able to leave a guard on her while we are gone," Amber said thinking they did not want to leave her alone in case Monahan came back to finish her in the hospital. Besides the two armed police officers, Josh Randal had sent two CIA field agents to provide backup to the officers.

"We need a car," Joanne said and then looked up and saw a man walking toward them. The man was limping, and used a cane for added support. He was being followed closely by a large German Shepherd dog that seemed to be smiling, with her tail wagging, and tongue out.

"Welcome to sunny, ah, well, snowy North Dakota. I am Brian Forest and this is Chilly, my partner. You may know our boss, Josh Randal and Tony Sanford," Brian said as he reached the small group.

"Isn't it kind of dangerous to be seen with us. We are known agents and you are undercover?" Joanne asked.

"Not undercover anymore. We have cleaned house; and the compound is now the property of the company and being turned into what is was designed to be. I am the interim guy in charge, with my faithful girl Friday here and my two-legged partner, Mona Vale," Brian said with a smile. "Come, I have a vehicle in the parking lot to take us home."

"Wow, that's a switch," Charlie said to nobody in particular.

"Well, it all changed just a few hours ago. I will explain on the way back," Brian said.

Back in Hawaii, Connie Pierce was fighting for her life. It was a matter of time and the waiting was equally as hard. Her wounds were severe. The planned heart transplant might allow her to survive. But they could not do the transplant until two things happened. First, they needed a new healthy heart which was hard to locate on the small island; and second, even with a healthy heart, they could not operate until she was strong enough to survive the procedure. It was the old catch 22 scenario; can't operate without a heart and can't operate until she was stronger. Both were going against her. The doctors and nurses continued to work around the clock to help her get stronger while they had hundreds looking for a healthy heart.

"While you were enjoying the flight from Hawaii, a lot changed in the world," Brian started to say as they exited the parking lot. Chilly sat in the back with her head on the back of the rear seat looking forward at Brian. He was interrupted when Amber's cell phone started to ring.

Amber pulled out her phone and said, "It's Val in Hawaii; I need to take this, sorry." She accepted the call and put the phone to her ear and listened; her expression changed from a smile to sadness immediately. "Hold on, Val, let me put you on speaker; everyone needs to hear this."

"Hello everyone," Val said to the group over the cell phone and then continued without pausing for a response. "Without dragging this out, Monahan turned up on our doorstep a couple of hours ago; he is dead."

"Dead!" Josh yelled.

212

"Sorry, but a dark van pulled up in front of Five-O headquarters. His body was dumped on our steps, and the van sped off before we could respond. We located the van. It was empty and there were no prints; it had been torched. It was stolen from a family on the other side of the island."

"No clues as to who dumped him or killed him?" Josh asked quickly.

"None, he was shot in the head with a small caliber pistol. He also had two shots in his left shoulder but they had only slowed him down a bit," Val commented.

"Damn!" Amber said quietly. "Any word on mom?"

"Nothing new, still in a coma and fighting. The doctors are doing everything they can," Val said with noticeable sadness in her voice.

"Thank you, Val," Amber said; she pressed disconnect, looked directly at Josh, and said, "Whoever is responsible for Monahan being killed is the man we need to find and kill."

"Amber, we just can't kill him; bring him to justice, and have the courts put him away," Joanne said quickly trying to defuse the tension.

"Look, Joanne, Monahan killed our father and put mom in the hospital fighting for her life. The man that hired him does not deserve to live, we don't even know what else he is planning on doing," Amber shot back.

"Okay, I understand, Connie is a friend and I feel for you, but killing and destroying your life is not anything she would want. We will capture him, and put him away for a very long time in a deep dark hole," Joanne said. She looked at Brian, and quietly said to him, "A little support would be helpful."

"She is right, Amber and Josh; we will get him and he will pay," Brian spoke up and then turned the SUV north on the highway.

"How long till we get to the compound; and you still haven't told us what is happening in the world," Josh asked.

"Simply put, North Korea has declared war on us. The President is doing what he can to calm them down before anybody gets killed. All indications are the North Koreans are going to do first strike with weapons of mass destruction, ICBMs launched at us; and the sad thing is that over the past twenty years, they have been able to develop ICBMs that can reach the United States as far inland as St. Louis. They have also built several nuclear missile ships and submarines. We have, hopefully, located all of those ships and subs and are ready to take them out if they fire at us. The president does not want to start the war, but he is committed to ending it quickly."

"Wow, so is that why your partner is back at the compound?" Josh asked.

"Yes, I will show you everything when we get there. The compound is not just a hospital, but, well, a lot more which I can't talk about here. I have already said more than I should in an unsecure vehicle."

Three hours later and after a short stop for fuel, rest room break, and snacks, they arrived at the gate to the North Dakota compound. Brian pressed a button on what looked like his cell phone and the gate opened.

"Welcome to North Dakota, home of Site Six," Brian stated as he drove through and continued down the dirt road toward a ranch house in the distance.

"Site Six?" Charlie piped in after sitting quietly for hours.

"Heard of it?" Brian asked.

"Yes and no. I have been to Site Four; and if this is anything like it, I am impressed," Charlie replied.

"They are similar, Charlie. But let's not talk about them until we are safely down below," Brian asked.

"Roger that, big man," Charlie agreed.

Forty minutes after passing through the gate, they were riding down the elevator to the secret control room two hundred feet below the surface. Nobody said a word as they rode down.

"Okay, I have been authorized by my brother, the President, to show you a few things that are way above your security clearance. What you are about to see is highly classified and you will not discuss this with anyone above this floor. We are presently about two hundred feet below the surface. I say about, because when it snows upstairs, we are actually much deeper. The main facility is no deeper than ninety feet down. This area was built as a nuclear bomb shelter, and then modified during the construction of the main facility above us," Brian said just as the elevator stopped. The numbers on the panel stopped at six, but the elevator continued on down below and showed no indication of going deeper; but yet it continued down.

"Okay, you have our word; we won't talk, but, well, I guess you are about to tell us what this is all about," Joanne said for the group.

Amber, Joanne, Josh, Charlie, Brian and Chilly stepped out of the elevator to be greeted by Mona Vale standing in the hall with her arms crossed and a pissed off look on her face.

"What took you guys so long. I was getting lonely down here. We just received a message from your brother," Mona said as they exited. "So sorry about your dad and mom. Anything I can do to help, please let me know."

"We're fine, Mona. Pleasure to meet you," Amber said remembering Brian had mentioned her name in the SUV. Josh stood silent and just stared at Mona. She was beautiful in a rugged sort of way.

"Don't get any ideas, Josh. Besides being my partner, she is my girl," Brian said quietly to Josh as they walked into the hall. "This way everyone; and this is Mona Vale, my two-legged partner and future wife," he announced as he led them down the hall to the only door at the end. Chilly looked up at him as if saying *'Hey, I am your girl.'*

"What did big brother have to say?" Brian asked as he stopped at the door to punch in the code to enter.

"He said keep your head down and watch the scopes; the North Koreans will not step down. They are prepared for war and nothing he has said will convince them to back down," Mona said just as he opened the door.

"Come on in; this may be our home for a while, at least mine and Mona's. You may be leaving soon, but need to know what is going on," Brian said and then waved them in.

"Wow, looks like the bridge of a star ship," Josh commented.

"Yeah, just like Site Four, thought it would be the same," Charlie said.

"There are six total sites identical to this one scattered around the country. Each is manned or rather has a team to monitor and activate the systems if needed during an attack. We have radar and complete control of four laser guns that are mounted in four of the spare silos upstairs. When we built this place, only eight of the silos were converted to sleeping quarters. The other four were converted to hold laser guns that would rise to the surface and lock on incoming missiles with the purpose of destroying said missiles. They can be used to take out aircraft or drones too. Years ago, we had the Patriot system which used missiles to knock out targets; now we use high powered lasers."

"I am confused. Why are we, two CIA agents and two kids of CIA agents, here? We really don't have the need to know about this," Joanne questioned.

"Well, that is where you are wrong. The reason you are being shown this is simple. The man you are looking for helped develop those lasers and put them in place. He knows the systems inside and out and wants to take control of them to make sure they

216

are not used when North Korea attacks. We do have one other ace in the hole as it were. Orbiting around our great planet in a stationary orbit are four Star Wars type laser systems. They are controlled by NORAD, but can be controlled from this site. If he has control of these, the United States will not be able to stop any incoming missiles or enemy aircraft. Now you know why you have to stop him."

"Yeah, but we don't know where he is. Can this equipment help us locate him?" Joanne asked.

"No it can't. But we do believe Rocky Soto is behind the attack on the Prime Minister," Brian stated.

Chapter 42 Blood Lines

"Come in, son," Rocky said when he answered the door to the penthouse at the top of the Regency Hotel in Bombay, India.

"Thanks, father. Do you have anything to drink?" Horatio asked as he walked in and laid his suitcase down by the door.

"Sure, you know where the bar is; help yourself," Rocky replied, turned, walked over to the sofa, and sat, staring at the TV. The news was on and he just heard the report that the North Koreans had declared war on the United States. No attacks had happened, but troops were staging all over the Demilitarized Zone on both sides.

After getting his drink, Horatio walked over, sat across from his dad, and sipped his drink, staring.

"Why are you here, Horatio?" Rocky finally said when a commercial came on.

"Well, I heard from my pilot that you were injured during that attack on the PM, and I was concerned," he lied. "And I needed a place to leave a small package that I picked up in L.A."

"Son, don't bull shit me. I know you were behind that attack. I just don't know why. I thought we were working toward the same thing. Why did you do it?" Rocky demanded to know. "And what is this package you want to leave here?"

"Why? You ask, why? You should know why. That North Korean is not to be trusted. After you contacted him about the lasers and set up the meet, he contacted me and asked for the hit to take place. He wanted it to look like the American CIA were involved; and as it were, several agents were killed and identified at the hotel. We did lose a couple of good men too, but they also carried CIA identification. He paid us three million dollars to plan and execute the hit. When I directed the attack, you were not supposed to be hurt, but accidents happen. I am just happy you are all right. However, the PM wanted you dead, because he thought he could get all the information about the lasers from me and cut you out."

"Thank you for the confession. Now, about the next step in our plan, do you still have anyone at Site Six and the other sites?" Rocky asked. "And again, where is the package?"

"Yes, we have been able to get into each compound, but not able to get to the control room. We will get there soon," Horatio admitted. "The package will be here soon. Right now, she is being held in a suite down the hall. I did not want her to hear our conversation. I have two men guarding her, and she is cooperating at the moment. I have informed the President that we have her. At a future time, I will call back to tell him what he needs to do to get her back."

"Soon doesn't work. We need them in now," Rocky said, but did not show much concern.

"When is the meet with the ISIS guys?" Horatio asked.

"Tonight, at nine."

"Do you want me there?"

"No, I want you to fly back to North Dakota and take control of the laser battery there. Once you have that, activate it, and destroy the satellite lasers. I built in a backdoor that will allow you to take control of all six sites. Kill anyone that gets in your way, especially that Brian Forest. He is presently in charge of the compound and most likely working with one of the alphabet organizations."

"No problem, father. He works directly for the President as a member of the Secret Service," Horatio commented smiling. "How did you... no never mind. Secret Service, well that answers a lot of questions. Kill him," Rocky ordered. "Now I need to get ready to meet with our new friends. Your room is that one over there; get settled in, and leave first thing in the morning. By the way, I have asked for a couple of ladies to join us tonight. They should arrive around eight; keep them happy until I return."

"No problem, father. Did you order dinner too? I am starving."

"Yes, should be up in a few minutes," Rocky said.

"Come on in," Horatio said when he answered the knock on the door and found a female pushing a cart full of food. He directed it to the table across the room, tipped her fifty dollars, and smiled as she left. "Dinner is here, father."

After a great dinner, Rocky left to meet with ISIS and the North Koreans. If all went as planned, he and Horatio would be set for life. Horatio sat on the sofa and turned on the TV.

"Well ,hello, come on in," Horatio said to the two beautiful oriental women who had just knocked on his door.

"Mr. Soto, I am Vanessa; and this is my good friend Jasmine," Vanessa said as they walked into the room. Both were dressed in very tight short skirts and blouses that accented their ample breasts, neither one had a bra on under their blouse.

"Care for a drink, ladies?" Horatio asked as he closed the door behind them. They all walked over to the sofa and the ladies sat, both smiling.

"Sure, scotch on the rocks if you have some," Vanessa said in a very sexy voice. "Is Rocky here?"

"No, but he will return soon. I am Horatio, his son."

"Nice, a father and son, Jasmine, you get the father, this young stud is mine," she said as she stood, took the glass from Horatio, and kissed him passionately hard on the lips.

Rocky was sitting across from the two members of ISIS and two North Korean representatives discussing a trade.

"Gentlemen, do we have an agreement?" Rocky asked the four.

"Mr. Soto, when can we expect delivery of the bomb that you promised?" The tall dark ISIS man that called himself Barrack said.

"There will be no delivery, when we attempted to retrieve the warhead it, well, let's just say it is long gone. I am sorry that you travelled so far for nothing," Rocky stated knowing that telling these people that he failed meant that they would kill him as soon as they could, just not here and now. They did not want to kill the two Koreans, but Rocky was a marked man.

"Mr. Soto, watch your back. Unless you can produce a bomb for us by the end of the week, you will be dead," Barrack said as he stood and both ISIS participants left the meeting.

"Failing those two has put you in a pretty bad position, Mr. Soto. You could not provide them with what they want, yet you say you can provide us with the plans and operational specifications for high power laser weapons. When can you provide these plans and specifications?" a North Korean representative going by the name John asked.

"John, I designed the weapons and will provide them as soon as I get assurance that your country will transfer a hundred million dollars into my account. I will also assist your engineers in the construction of the weapons. I promise they will perform as stated and we can produce them within two weeks if you have acquired all the material I have requested."

"We have the material and engineers standing by. Will you fly back with us to start the project?" John asked.

"Yes, as soon as the money is in my account," Rocky agreed.

"Are you worried they will be waiting for you just outside?" John asked, pointing to the door.

"No, because they are already dead; well, not yet, but soon. They need to report back to their bosses; and, of course, they will do it in person, not by using the technology known as a phone. They will fly back, and during the flight their plane will have a nasty accident. There will be no survivors," Rocky said smiling, knowing that his team had already eliminated both ISIS members.

"We leave in the morning. Meet us at the airport at ten. Don't be late and bring the plans," John said and both men left.

Rocky walked out of the restaurant and returned to his penthouse to find Jasmine sitting patiently on the sofa. He did not see Horatio or the other escort, but heard noise coming from Horatio's room.

"Hello, I am Rocky and you are?"

"Jasmine, shall we..." she said pointing to his bedroom.

"I need a drink, and then we shall..." he agreed.

Chapter 43 Hawaiian Vacation

After getting the nickel tour of the compound, seeing everything that mattered, and some things that didn't matter, Joanne and her team were well rested and impressed with what Brian and his team had completed.

"Brian this is a very impressive facility, and I know it will be put to good use. But…" Joanne commented as they sat across from him in the galley. "But, there is always a but, the two of you can't be on call twenty-four seven. Is your brother sending help?"

"Yes, he is; you and Charlie have been assigned here to assist me and Mona."

"What, we have to go after Rocky Soto and his team," Joanne protested.

"That has been put on hold for now. Tony and Josh Randal concur that until we have some solid information as to where they are, you will stay here. Tony has activated a reserve company trained in lasers and combat to report here in three days. Until they arrive, you are my back-up," Brian ordered.

"Well, I guess if the President and our boss says to stay, then we stay. What about Josh and Amber, are they staying?" Charlie stated.

"No, they are to return to Hawaii to be with their mother; she needs them there. They leave in the morning. The pilots have been briefed, and will be ready to fly at noon. I have a helicopter chartered to fly out here to pick them up at nine."

"Guess they won the Hawaiian vacation and we got North freaking Dakota," Joanne said quietly.

"Hey, it isn't bad here, except in the winter when we have eight feet of snow on the ground and can't get around very well," Brian stated.

"Have a safe trip back, and let us know how your mom is doing," Joanne said to Amber and Josh as they waited for the helicopter to land. Joanne reached over and gave each one a hug.

"Be careful Joanne," Josh said. "With a war on the horizon, this place could very well become a target."

"It may be a target, but we will be deep underground. Even a nuclear explosion right on top of us should only give us a headache. At least, that is all it is supposed to do anyway," Brian stated.

"Still, stay safe, all of you," Amber said quietly.

"We will, and you too," Charlie said and then helped them board the helicopter.

An hour later, they were sitting in the Gulfstream waiting for the pilot to taxi out and take off. They each had a drink, Josh a beer and Amber an orange juice.

"You still have your weapon, Amber?" Josh asked as they started to taxi out.

"Yes, do you? Did you call Val and tell her when we would be back?"

"Of course, she said she would be there when we land and take us to the safe house. She also said she would have a couple of uniform officers staying at the safe house while we are there, just in case," Amber commented between sips of her orange juice.

"Good, I want to go straight to the hospital and check on mom," Josh insisted.

"For sure, little brother," Amber agreed.

"I am not your little brother; I was born one minute before you which makes me the older, big brother. Ha, ha!" Josh countered.

"My brother, you will always be my little brother; maybe not in age or size, but in my mind, you will always be my little brother," Amber stated.

"Ok, my little sister, we need to come up with a plan to catch this guy; stop him from causing any more damage," Josh said and then leaned back to think.

"Well, we do have a few hours to kill, about eight from what the pilot says," Amber said and then picked up her drink. "The service is terrible on this flight; where is that steward?" she said as she reached up to press the call button but could not find one. "Where's the button?"

"Little sister, this is not a commercial jet. Remember, we have to help ourselves," Josh said. He stood up, walked to the galley, and helped himself to another beer and a can of orange juice for Amber.

Eight and a half hours later, the Gulfstream touched down in Honolulu and taxied to the General Aviation terminal. While looking out the window, Amber said, "There's Val with three other people I don't recognize."

"Must be our chaperones," Josh said. He stood after the jet stopped and the door was opened by the co-pilot. They walked down the steps and were greeted by Val.

"Welcome back to Hawaii; did you enjoy the short rest in North Dakota?" Lieutenant Valerie Lake asked as they walked to the car.

"Good trip, learned a lot from Joanne and Charlie. What happened with Monahan?" Amber said.

"He was shot in the head and dumped on our door step. No leads, found the van he was dumped from, only his blood inside, no finger prints or anything we could use. If we only had Abby here to help, she always found a clue when nobody else could," Val stated.

"Abby, who is this Abby?" Amber questioned.

"Don't you watch NCIS? Abby is their Forensic Scientist and is damn good. If we had her, we could crack this case wide open," Val said with a smile.

"Oh, that Abby. Yeah, I watch NCIS and she is hot," Josh replied. "I catch all the re-runs and wow."

"Come on, we need to get to the safe house. Have you two had dinner?" Val asked.

"No, how about some Italian," Josh said.

"No way, Jose. Too fattening. Chinese or a salad for me," Amber said quickly.

"We have a cook at the safe house who will fix you anything you want."

"We need to stop at the hospital first, if you don't mind," Amber insisted.

"Sure, hospital, then safe house, and dinner," Val agreed and steered the car toward the hospital. Her three officers followed in the car behind them.

The visit to the hospital was not productive. Connie was resting, but still in a coma, not much improvement, but still alive. The hospital had not located a healthy heart, but was not giving up.

"Let's go," Amber said and kissed her mother on the forehead. Josh leaned over and kissed his mom and they left the room, stopping to talk to the doctor on duty for a moment. She agreed to call them, if there was any change, no matter what time it was.

Chapter 44 The Dark Side

Down in the Autopsy Department of Honolulu General Hospital, Doctor Lance Nesbit was looking over the recent requests from organs that could be used from the numerous organ donors he had on file. The list was long, and if he had a donor, he could comply; but business was light, and he had only four possible candidates in his department. Two were donors as indicated by their charts and personal requests, but neither were for any or all organs. One was for eyes and the other for anything needed to help someone survive.

"Damn, not a match," he said to himself as he scanned the donor list and then the request list. "What is the status of that gunshot victim?" he yelled over to his young assistant, Mary Wilson.

"Type A positive blood, looks like a healthy heart, liver not so good, too much alcohol and bad food," Mary replied as she examined the internal organs of George Monahan.

"Is the heart healthy?" Nesbit asked looking up from the list; he had just seen the urgent request for a healthy heart for a gunshot victim, upstairs.

"He's been dead for ten hours, but the heart looks undamaged," Mary yelled back across the room.

"Remove it and prep for transfer," Nesbit said and then stood, rushed over to prep himself for surgery, stopped for a second and picked up his desk phone. He called the Intensive Care Unit.

"Good morning, ICU," the nurse on duty said as she answered her phone.

"This is Nesbit in autopsy. I think I have a healthy heart for the patient Connie Pierce," he said speaking very fast. "We are about to extract and prep for transfer. I will advise when it is ready."

"That is great; I will notify Doctor Gentry," the nurse responded.

Nesbit hung up the phone and immediately prepped for surgery.

"Call the Pierce kids; we need their permission to do the transfer," Doctor Gentry ordered his nurse. "I will be in with Pierce," he stated and then walked down the hall to the cubicle where Connie was resting; she was still in a coma and not getting any better.

"Already called them. They will be in here shortly," Nurse King replied and then turned back to monitoring her station.

Forty minutes later, Amber, Josh and Val Lake walked into the ICU. "What's the emergency?" Amber asked as soon as they reached the desk with Nurse King.

"We are not sure, but we believe we have a donor for your mother," Nurse King said and then added, "Doctor Gentry will have more information." Then she paged Gentry.

Minutes later, a tall well-tanned man dressed in hospital whites walked up and directed them to the waiting room.

"What do you know, doctor?" Josh asked without waiting to enter the waiting room. Luckily the room was empty so they could talk freely.

"Please take a seat," Doctor Gentry said and then sat down across from the three. "Nurse King probably told you that we possibly have a healthy heart for your mother. There are some complications which you need to know; and, of course, since she is in a coma, you have to authorize the surgery. First, we have done hundreds of heart transplants over the years. I personally have completed sixty-seven successful transplants."

"That is impressive, doctor, but what are you not telling us?" Amber questioned.

"The heart we have is from another shooting victim; he died over nine hours ago. This complicates the transfer. The heart is healthy, but has not been in use for hours. We should be able to revive it, but there is always a chance that it will not restart. That is only part of the problem; and you need to understand, our goal is to get your mother back to good health."

"Wait, male gunshot victim, don't tell me, it's not George Monahan; please don't let it be him," Amber jumped in quickly.

"Yes, it is Monahan," Doctor Gentry answered.

"No way, doctor, putting the heart of the man that killed my father and shot my mother. No way," Josh yelled.

"Son, she could die without the transplant. We can't wait much longer; this heart is healthy and available. Well, we think it is available; we haven't contacted his next of kin, but may just have to break the rules to save her," Gentry added.

"I don't know if our mom could live knowing the heart that saved her is from the man that almost killed her," Amber said calmly.

"That may not be a problem, if we don't get permission from his next of kin. We located, in his cell phone, the number of a sister in Tulsa, Oklahoma. We have called and left a message for her to call us. Hopefully, she will call; and we can send her the authorization paperwork. Without it, we can't legally use the heart," Gentry said but not smiling.

"How much time do we have to decide, doc?" Josh asked.

"Four hours, after that the chances of using that heart declines," Gentry replied sadly.

"Will she live without the transplant?" Amber questioned.

"She has a fifty-fifty chance. Could go either way."

Chapter 45 North Korean Con

Rocky and Horatio parted early the next morning; both were tired but happy. The two ladies were well worth the money they paid them. They were hot, sexy and had a lot of energy and that was before they undressed and were in bed. Once in bed, the two Sotos had been treated to things that they had never experienced before. The ladies left happy and tired too, but also a bit richer. The night of decadence cost Rocky one thousand dollars, but he felt it was well worth it.

"Father, are you really going to North Korea?" Horatio asked as they placed their travel bags beside the door for the bell cap to pick up.

"Yes, but they are not getting what they have paid for, something better," Rocky responded. "What are you going to do with the little lady down the hall?"

"Don't screw with these guys, that PM is a nut case. He'd just as soon kill you than to give you what you want," Horatio pleaded.

"Yes, but he will never get the chance. Remember my little holographic projector; well, I have two with me. Once I get the project going, I will initiate a little accident that will destroy their lab and kill all the engineers there. My body will be among the dead, only it will not be me. I will have been long gone with the material I need to build my own system to use against the Americans. And the best part is that they will build it for me."

"Don't do it, father. The Americans are searching for us now; and if they find you working with the North Koreans, your life will not be worth spit," Horatio said and then opened the door for the bellhop.

"You worry too much my young son. I have this under control. Now don't you have business back in the States? And you need to do something with your package down the hall," Rocky said and then headed for the door.

"Yes, and my plane is waiting; so is yours," replied Horatio. "Don't worry about her, she is just a little guarantee that Mr. Sanford will do what I say.

Two hours later, Horatio's plane departed Bombay bound for Hawaii and then on to Los Angeles. The president's daughter rode quietly in the back of the cabin, doing what she was told and not complaining.

At the same time, Rocky was on a North Korean private jet heading northeast toward North Korea. Rocky was playing with fire. His plan was to assist the North Korean engineers in the construction of what they thought would be the control unit to a laser defense system; but, in reality, with the material he had them get together to build it, they were actually going to construct a bomb. Rocky was going to steal it, and leave the country as quickly as possible.

The type of bomb he had designed did not destroy buildings or infrastructure but instead only killed anything that relied on air to survive. Similar bombs had been constructed earlier, but failed to do what he wanted. If successful, his bomb would only kill and not destroy. However, to build it, he needed some components that he could not get. These unobtainable components were highly controlled elements that could only be acquired by governments or one of their organizations. Since he was no longer attached to any legitimate government, his only option was to convince or trick a government to get the required elements for him.

After getting out of North Korea with the bomb, he planned on detonating it in Washington DC. This would be the ultimate terrorist attack and all the files, money and resources would be available for him and his team to take over the government. The bomb was something out of the twenty-fourth century, similar to a disruptor or phasor set on vaporize, as all carbon-based lifeforms would just vaporize when the bomb detonated. The bomb only destroyed living tissue. He had discovered the proper formula while working in the lab at CIA. When he was fired, he took the formula and continued to work and test it. No clean up required, no bodies and no total destruction, if it worked as planned. He did have to be careful; the range was estimated to be about four square miles, weakening to a max range of six square miles. Anyone in that area would just disappear and those on the fringe would experience symptoms similar to the flu and die within days.

Horatio just wanted to catch up to that woman who had become part of his inner circle making him believe she was someone she wasn't. He didn't know who or where she was, but was determined to find her somehow. Horatio did not know what his father had designed, and really didn't want to know. Using the president's daughter, he would be able to trade her for that woman. He had no reason to harm the President's daughter, but many reasons to kill Joanne, or whatever name she was using now. Once back in the States, he would tell the President what he wanted and make the trade.

Chapter 46 Going the Distance

"Hello, this is Nurse King in ICU, may I speak with either Amber or Josh Pierce?" Nurse King asked over the phone.

"This is Amber, Miss King. Is everything all right with my mom?" Amber asked quickly.

"Yes, the doctor asked me to call you to ask if you and your brother would come back to the hospital as soon as you can," Nurse King asked.

"Sure, we will be right there; is my mom okay?" Amber asked again.

"Your mom is fine. Doctor Gentry needs to speak with you; please come on in," Nurse King insisted.

"On our way," Amber responded and then disconnected the call. "Josh we have to go. Is Val still here?"

"No, she had go back to the station. Is something wrong?" Josh asked. He then walked over to the phone, called down to the officer in the lobby, and asked for a car and driver to take them to the hospital.

Twenty-five minutes later, Amber and Josh were walking into the ICU followed by a young police officer, assigned to their protection.

"What is going on, Nurse?" Amber asked as they approached the desk.

"Just a moment, Miss Pierce; I will get Doctor Gentry to talk to you. Would you take a seat in the waiting room?" the Nurse said.

"We will wait right here if you don't mind," Josh said being a bit harsher than he meant to be. "Sorry."

"He will be here in a few minutes; you may be more comfortable..." Nurse King said, but stopped when she saw Doctor Gentry walking down the hall toward them.

"Glad you could come in; would you come with me," Gentry said and immediately turned and started back the way he had come, stopping in front of the door for their mother's room. "Come on in; someone wants to see you."

"She's awake!" Amber exclaimed as she rushed into the room to find her mother sitting up in bed smiling. "Mom!"

"Mom!" Josh said as he walked over to the bed behind Amber.

"Hi kids," Connie said weakly. "I am glad you came."

"Mom, how do you feel?" Amber asked.

"I hurt like hell, but the drugs are toning that down. How are you two doing?" Connie asked.

"I will leave you three alone, but not too long; she is still very weak," Doctor Gentry said and started to leave the room when Amber turned and grabbed him, giving him a huge hug.

"Thank you, doc; is she going to be okay?" Amber asked.

"All indications are that she will recover, but her heart is still damaged. We need to discuss what to do next. Visit first and talk over the heart we have with your mom before any decisions are made," Gentry said, "I will be back in ten minutes."

"Thank you, doc," Josh said quickly.

"What's that talk about my heart?" Connie asked in a very weak voice.

"Mom, one of the bullets damaged your heart. They are monitoring it and are hoping the damage will heal itself, but are not sure it will. If it doesn't get better soon, you may need a heart transplant," Josh told his mom.

"Okay, if I need a new heart, they need to find one and put it in, if needed," Connie agreed, pausing for a second then said, "Don't they have artificial hearts made with those 3D printers that work just fine?"

"Yes, they have the artificial hearts; but if a real heart is available, the doctors prefer them over the manufactured one. They have a real heart right now that is healthy and is a match, but there is a problem."

"A problem, what kind of problem?" asked their Mom.

"Ah, I am not sure you want to know. Maybe we are being too overly dramatic, but you need to know," Amber said trying not to tell her, but knowing they had to.

"What have we taught you kids? If there is a problem, solve it and move on. What is the problem? Spit it out! Don't make me get out of the bed," Connie said with a smile and a little laugh. "Oh, don't make me laugh; it hurts."

"Josh you tell her," Amber said to her brother. "You are the oldest, and my big brother, so it is your responsibility."

"Wait a sec, little sister, that is not what you said yesterday. Okay, I will..." Josh said, when she punched him on the arm.

"Cut it out and just tell me," Connie almost yelled, but grimaced in pain instead.

"Mom, the man that shot you, George Monahan, was killed and dumped on the door step of the police station. His heart is a match to you and they are proposing to use his heart in you. We were not sure if that would set well with you," Josh said seriously. After pausing to take a breath, he added, "If they have to do the transplant, they prefer a real heart over the artificial."

"Wow, the man that killed your father and almost, well may have killed me, is possibly going to save my life by giving me his heart. That is unreal," Connie said quietly, slowly taking in everything her kids had just told her.

"It is not positive; the hospital has to get a release from his sister in Oklahoma before they can do the surgery. And, keep in mind, you may not need it. You are awake now; and with luck, you will not need the transplant. But it is your decision, not ours, now that you are awake and can make that decision yourself."

"If it is my decision, then I decide, well, let me think about it... Take that heart and bury it..." Connie said quietly.

Chapter 47 Is This the End

Two weeks after Rocky Soto arrived in North Korea, he made his escape. Along with the device he designed and built with the help of the now deceased Korean engineers, he made his way to the coast where he was picked up, by his team, on a small, but fast, submarine. His destination was Washington DC to finish his plan.

Meanwhile, Horatio had arrived in Hawaii to confirm that his men had completed their task of eliminating George Monahan.

"Good afternoon, Morris. Did you complete the mission?" the old, oriental gentleman asked when he sat down across from Edward Morris in the small coffee shop just off the beach.

"Yes, sir, just as promised," Morris replied.

"Good, good. Your payment has been transferred to your account in the Caymans. I hope you enjoy the little bonus I added," the old man said quietly. "Is the coffee good here?"

"Yes, they only use Kona coffee, roasted daily," Morris replied.

"Would you be so kind as to get me a cup, black is fine?"

"Sure, no problem, be right back," Morris said and then stood, walked over to the counter, placed the order, paid for it, and upon returning to the table said, "They will bring it right over, sir."

"Thank you. I have one more task for you. The details are in this envelope; your fee will be the same as last time, half in the envelope and the balance in your account. There is a ticket for you to fly to Los Angeles and then on to Washington DC. You are to complete this task, by the time you reach Washington. If you fail, well, I will not be able to pay you the balance," the old man said.

"If I do this, I expect to get paid," Morris said sternly.

"Oh, you will get paid, if you succeed; but if you fail, you most likely will be dead," the old man replied with a small smile.

"Dead."

"Yep, dead. You see the person you need to see is my father and he is very dangerous. You know what they say about geniuses don't you?"

"No, what do they say?"

"There is a very fine line between genius and insanity and he has been walking that line for months and needs to be stopped before he hurts someone else," the old man said quietly then stopped when his coffee arrived. "Thank you, miss," he said and handed her a hundred-dollar bill as a tip.

"Thank you sir," she replied with a big smile.

"When do I leave?" Morris asked.

"The red eye tonight, eleven-fifteen," the old man said and then paused for a second before continuing, "I also must warn you, I have tipped off the FBI that he is coming and is carrying a weapon of mass destruction. I don't care who stops him; you will get paid if you are still alive," he said and then sipped his coffee, "Yes, excellent coffee, thank you."

A half hour later, Horatio was walking toward his hotel located two blocks from the coffee shop. He knew he was being followed, but that did not concern him. He had just put a contract out on his father, also knowing full well that Morris would not succeed. Horatio did not want his father dead; and his father did not want to be dead. The plan was to eliminate any connection between the contract killer and both he and his father. Rocky and Horatio had planned this, and Rocky had the trap set. Sure, Horatio could have killed Morris, but this was more fun.

Stopping at the entrance to the hotel, Horatio turned and looked at the man that was following him, smiled and winked. The man had stopped and looked directly at Horatio just as a car slammed on its brakes beside the man and opened fire with an automatic weapon, killing him instantly. Horatio smiled, the FBI had thought they could follow him, but he was smarter than the FBI. He had Morris follow at a safe distance to take out the agent.

Mr. Morris had done his job, but he had a plane to catch; his next assignment would be difficult to say the least. After speeding away from the scene, he drove directly to the airport, dropped his rental car off, and headed to his gate.

Killing Rocky Soto would be a challenge, but he was up to the challenge. His plane would leave Los Angeles at eleven fifteen this evening, and arrive around seven in the morning in Washington.

Horatio, slipped into the hotel, walked directly to the elevator, and stepped in. He was alone, so, as the elevator started to climb to his floor, he quickly deactivated his disguise on his portable holographic projector. When he stepped off the elevator on the third floor, he was a young man in a blue blazer. The old oriental gentleman had completely disappeared. He pressed the down button on the adjacent elevator, stood and waited for the door to open. He entered once it arrived, and was met by a beautiful brunette in a very short leather mini skirt, almost transparent blouse, four inch spiked heels and a smile that could melt butter. Beside her was a short, barrel chested man carrying a briefcase and wearing a nicely tailored, pin striped suit; he too was smiling.

"Good afternoon," Horatio said smiling at the lady and ignoring the man completely. He wondered if she were as expensive as she looked.

"Good afternoon," she said, flashing a full set of pure white teeth.

"Good afternoon, sir," the short gentleman said.

They all rode down to the lobby quietly and exited when the door opened. The young lady walked over to the lobby desk and spoke with the man behind before exiting the hotel.

"Who is that beautiful lady?" Horatio asked the desk clerk after watching her leave. He should have introduced himself to her in the elevator but wasn't sure of her connection with the other man. Hindsight is twenty-twenty and he just didn't see it at the time, thinking he might have been her father. Not a chance, she was a highly paid escort and most likely made enough off this short guy to pay for her apartment rent for a couple of months.

"I'm afraid I can't tell you that sir; we don't divulge our guests' names or any information to anyone unless we have a warrant from the police, or their permission. It is company policy, sir," the desk clerk said smiling, knowing full well who she was and why she was in the hotel. She did rent a room here and always paid cash.

"That's a good policy, is she a guest at this hotel? "

"Yes, she is, sir and that is about all I can tell you," the clerk said.

"Thank you," Horatio said and then walked out of the hotel, hoping to catch up to her; but no luck, she was gone. Time to call the FBI.

He pulled out the burn phone he had bought while he was still disguised as an old oriental man, and dialed the number from memory.

"Hello, may I speak with the head of department that deals with kidnapping," Horatio said speaking as an old man.

"Just a moment, sir," the reply came. Within a minute, a female voice answered.

"Sir, are you calling to report a kidnapping?" she asked.

"No, not exactly, I am calling because I am the kidnapper. Are you in charge?" he asked and then added, "You may trace this phone, but I will not be here long enough for you to find me. I have the President's daughter and would like to make a trade. Are you the one that can make this happen?"

"You have kidnapped the President's daughter and want to trade for what?" she asked as she signaled to her assistant to trace the call. She also wrote a note and handed it to one of her assistants that instructed her to call the White House.

"Yes, I have. I also have told your boss that I have her; he may have already informed the President. What I want is simple; a CIA female agent that posed as my girlfriend, humiliated me, and then attempted to kill a friend of mine. I want her in trade. I don't want to harm the President's daughter, but I want that woman. I will call again in eight hours to give you details for the trade. Good bye," Horatio said. He hung up the phone; and as he walked down the street, he pitched it into the waste can by the door to a hotel.

Horatio stopped on the corner and watched several police cars pull up to where the shooting had occurred not more than twenty minutes earlier. They were questioning witnesses; and when the police discovered the victim was an FBI agent, they immediately called their station and requested the FBI to come on the scene as soon as possible.

Horatio smiled, turned and started to walk away from the hotel. His plan was to stop for a drink, have a light dinner and get some sleep. Tomorrow, he was to meet with his father in Washington DC to set the last phase of their plan into motion. By the time he would arrive, Mr. Morris would be dead; and he would have just saved half a million dollars. Maybe he would use some of the savings to get himself a sexy lady for the evening.

'Yeah, that's what I will do. Here in Los Angeles there should be some ladies of the evening that would enjoy my company and a large bit of cash should ensure she will do as I ask,' Horatio thought.

If you enjoyed reading this book, you may want to check out other stories in the *Chain of Deceit* series by D.A. McIntosh, https://www.amazon.com/D.-A.-McIntosh/e/B0083OZK7S

Chain of Deceit, Book 1
Retribution, Book 2
T Minus 36, Book 3
Final Report, Book 4
Wounded Eagle, Book 5
Schutzstaffel Rising, Book 6

The Island
Target
Vengeance (coming soon)

Also, be on the lookout for each book on Audio book available on Amazon, Audible.com and iTunes

Reference Information

<table>
<tr><td colspan="2">Lat.: 9.3203° N
Long.: 73.8076° E</td><td colspan="3">Annular Solar Eclipse
Duration of Annularity: 5m26.1s
Magnitude: 0.979
Obscuration: 91.94%</td></tr>
</table>

Event	Date	Time (UT)	Alt	Azi
Start of partial eclipse (C1) :	2031/05/21	05:19:12.1	63.1°	063.4°
Start of annular eclipse (C2) :	2031/05/21	07:20:28.1	78.2°	337.5°
Maximum eclipse :	2031/05/21	07:23:11.0	77.9°	334.7°
End of annular eclipse (C3) :	2031/05/21	07:25:54.1	77.6°	332.0°
End of partial eclipse (C4) :	2031/05/21	09:25:39.4	53.6°	291.5°

The properties shown here are real and my story is based loosely on the first property. There many other similar sites around our country.

Rare Sprint Missile Site Northern North Dakota

Property Description

Own one of the rarest nuclear hardened underground structures in the world. This property was one of four Sprint Missile Sites located approximately 10-20 miles from a central radar control site. Constructed in the early 1970's, these bases were a last line of defense meant to intercept ICBMs coming over the North Pole. There was only one Safeguard Complex ever completed, making this unique property an incredibly rare opportunity. This property was in US Government possession from its construction until 2013, when it was purchased at GSA auction. During most of that time, it sat empty and neglected. It was also partially salvaged (ie. Valves, motors, generators, electronics electric cable have been removed). There is still a lot of steel conduit and I-beams to be removed and either reused or sold for scrap.

THE ACREAGE:
This property consists of 36 acres fenced. The inner fence around the missile field is 8' military grade chain anchored and ½" cable reinforced chain link fencing topped with barbed wire and the outer fence is ½" cable reinforced 4' wire fence. There is a paved patrol road around the inner fence perimeter. The property is well hidden from the main road by hills and is 2.5 miles from the nearest paved road. The property has wonderful drainage systems.
The site is located 8 miles from the nearest town of about 2,000. From the roof of the underground building you can see approximately 10 miles in every direction. It's a very defensible property!

The acreage is beautiful, rolling grasslands with two seasonal ponds (approx. 3 acres) which attract many birds including ducks and geese. Approximately one linear mile of trees was planted in 2013. The trees are a mix of cottonwood, linden, pine trees, and fruit bearing bushes. There are lots of local hunting and outdoor sporting opportunities year round.

Also on the property is a "missile field" that once contained 12 Sprint missiles that were ready for launch. They were housed in 12 steel missile tubes in the ground. Each tube is approximately 11' across and 35' deep.
A new water well was drilled in 2013 which supplies large quantities of water, but will need an RO system to ensure water is safe for drinking. As an alternative or redundant system, rural water is available within ¾ of a mile.

ABOVE-GROUND BUILDING:
The guardhouse is an above-ground, poured concrete, 2,400 square feet building complete with three garage bays, a kitchen, bathroom, office, and turnstile/security desk. This structure is heavily reinforced to withstand a nearby nuclear detonation. Electricity was reconnected in the summer of 2013 and the guardhouse has been professionally rewired and inspected including a new 200-amp service box. It has water systems, high efficiency propane central furnace and brand new propane hang up furnace in the garage bays both were installed in August of 2013.

The remodeled bathroom is functional with a brand new septic system, new hot water heater, new shower, new vanity/sink, and new toilet. The kitchen has a new refrigerator and is ready to install the brand new cabinets (included), and also plumbed for a propane stove (not included). Brand new, energy efficient windows have been purchased, but need to be installed. Although this structure has had a lot of updating, there is still work required to finish the renovation.

BELOW GROUND BUILDING:
The main structure on the property is the underground Launch Control Center which is naturally dry since it was built on a hill and has earth mounded over it. It consists of 12,000 square feet on one level with 15' ceilings and is divided into rooms of varying size by concrete walls. The outer walls are 30" thick and are heavily reinforced with large rebar.
Brand new electric service was professionally brought into the underground building including a large transfer switch suitable for hooking up a generator near the tunnel entrance and 2 new 200-amp service panels were installed, one at each end. A new septic system was installed for the underground building in addition to the one for the above ground building.

The structure is accessed via a 9'x9' square concrete tunnel, approximately 75' long that is usable for driving equipment in and out. At the bottom of the tunnel are 2 large blast doors for equipment and 2 smaller blast doors for personnel.
There are 2 large concrete towers above the structure. The shorter one is approximately 25' tall is the intake tower and the taller one, approximately 30', is the exhaust tower. These were originally used for the generator equipment.

Additionally, there are 2 heat sink buildings below grade. Each measures 20'x60' with 9' ceilings. These can be connected via tunnel to the underground bunker if desired. They would make ideal additional living or storage space.

Osage City, KS Atlas E site
Property Description

The Atlas E is usually considered the best ICBM site for retrofit with its drive-in access and over-all size. There were only 27 built. This Atlas E site is the last undeveloped site we know of for sale. It is located in rural pastoral setting of NE Kansas makes it a secluded and quiet get-a-way. The structure cost taxpayers $3,300,000 to construct (1960's dollars). Millions of dollars of concrete structure remain on site for use. This is a rare and historic property with much potential - clean-up necessary.

Features Include:

- 25 acres' m/l
- paved access
- rural water and electrical on site ready for re-connection
- sewer lagoon system is functional - needs new ejector pump
- barbed wire fence perimeter
- 15,000 sq. ft. of hardened underground floor-space - needs clean up and refurbishment
- overhead door, drive-in door and all 4 blast doors in place
- Grass landing strip

Weapons
M24 (American)

Calibre:	7.62x51mm NATO (.308 win)
Operation:	Bolt Action
Feed:	5-Round internal magazine
Weight:	12.1 lb (5.49 kg) empty without telescope
Length:	43in (1092mm)
Sights:	10×42 Leupold Ultra M3A telescope sight (Mil-Dots), plus detachable emergency iron sights. (Redfield Palma International)
Barrel:	416R Stainless Steel, 24″ length, 1:11.2″ twist, 5 radial land grooves
Stock:	HS Precision – adjustable length.
Max Effective Range:	800 meters (875 yards)
Expected Accuracy:	1 MOA with M118 .5 MOA with M118LR

The M24 Sniper's Weapon System (SWS) represents a return to bolt action sniper rifles by the US Army. As in the USMC M40A1, the M24 uses the Remington 700 action, although the reciever is a long action made for adaptation to take the .300 Winchester Magnum round. The stock (HS Precision) is made of a composite of Kevlar, graphite and fibreglass bound together with epoxy resins, and features an aluminium bedding block and adjustable butt plate. A detachable bipod (Harris) can be attached to the stocks fore-end. The metal finish is powder coated for extreme durability.

The rifle had a very quick development cycle as the US Army had decided it wanted to get snipers back into the US Army and was in the process of developing the B4 identifier and the school to award it. There was a major short fall of M21s, the standard sniper rifle, at that point of time and the Army figured it would need 10,000 sniper rifles of which they didn't have nearly that many M21s. So a new sniper rifle was developed at the same time and it was done in a record 22 months. The Weapon System Matrix Manager for the M24 was Major John Mende and he explains that the long action actually had nothing to do with the ability to convert to a .300 Win Mag but was a product of that quick development time. The rifle was intended to be chambered in the .30-06 as the -06 was a type classified ammunition for the Army unlike the .300 WM at the time. They wanted to have a high power load for the .30-06 eventually developed. As development of the system was moving forward they discovered that there was not enough .30-06 ammo in a single lot in the Army's inventory to test and develop the system so they quickly changed to the 7.62x51mm NATO (308 Win) and left the action the same as there was not enough time for the manufacturers of the stock and floor plate to make the change to short action. They also fully believed they would later do a product improvement update and convert all the M24s to .30-06. The fact that they could convert them to .300 Win Mag was an unexpected benefit to the SF groups and was never actually designed into the system.

Barrett .50 Cal (American)

Type	Sniper rifle
Place of origin	United States

Manufacturer	Barrett Firearms Company
Unit cost	$3800-$4000
Specifications	
Weight	25 lb (11.36 kg)
Length	50.4 in (1280 mm)
Barrel length	32 inches (813 mm)
Cartridge	.50 BMG (12.7 × 99 mm), .416 Barrett
Action	Single Shot, Bolt Action
Maximum range	2600 Meters

M4 Carbine

The **M4 carbine** is a shorter and lighter variant of the M16A2 assault rifle. The M4 is a 5.56×45mm NATO, air-cooled, direct impingement gas-operated, magazine-fed carbine. It has a 14.5 in (370 mm) barrel and a telescoping stock.

The M4 carbine is heavily used by the United States Armed Forces and is replacing the M16 rifle in most United States Army and United States Marine Corps combat units as the primary infantry weapon.[5][6]

The M4 is also capable of mounting the M203 grenade launcher. The distinctive step in their barrel is for mounting the M203 with the standard hardware. The **M4** is capable of firing in semi-automatic and three-round burst (like the M16A2 and M16A4), while the **M4A1** is capable of firing in semi-auto and full automatic (like the M16A1 and M16A3).

Colt M4 carbine, current issue model with removable carrying handle, left side

THOR Global Defense Group TR-15 carbine, manufactured along
the lines of US GI M4, but fitted with a number of accessories
such as AAC silencer, Vltor rail forend and buttstock, and
Trijicon ACOG 4X optical sight
image: THOR Global Defense Group

Type 68 pistol (Democratic People's Republic of Korea / North Korea)

Source: http://world.guns.ru/handguns/hg/nkor/type-6-e.html

Type	Single Action semiautomatic
Caliber(s)	7.62x25mm TT
Weight unloaded	795 g
Length	185 mm
Barrel length	108 mm
Magazine capacity	8 rounds

This pistol has been developed at state arms factories of DPRK by late 1960s, and is now in use with North Korean army. It is based on Soviet Tokarev TT, but with certain modifications. This pistol is rarely seen outside of DPRK.

Type 68 pistol is a short recoil operated, locked breech pistol. It uses a modified Browning type locking, with the barrel engaging the notches inside the slide with two lugs, machined on the top of the barrel. To lock and unlock upon the recoil cycle, breech end of the barrel is controlled by the cam-shaped cut in the underbarrel lug (instead of the swinging link, found in the original TT pistols). Trigger is of single action type, with exposed hammer. There is no manual safety, except for a half-cock notch on the hammer. Single stack magazines hold 8 rounds, and are slightly different from TT magazines, by not having the notch on the left side for a TT-type magazine catch. The magazine catch is located at the bottom of the grip. Standard TT magazines still can be used in Type 68 pistols, but not vice versa. Sights are of fixed type, with the rear sight dovetailed into slide.

VZ-61 Skorpion   .

The Czechoslovakian made VZ61 machine pistol is reportedly still in use by covert operatives of the North Korean government. These were obtained at various times in the 1960s, 1970s, and possibly 1980s, and have the standard grey paint finish, with 10 and 20 round magazines. Caliber is 7.65 Browning (.32 ACP). These have a high rate of fire, are very concealable, and when the suppressor is used, very quiet. The most recent event in which a Skorpion was found was in 1998, when the dead body of North Korean spy with diver gear was found on a South Korean beach.

US Navy Destroyers

Dec. 18, 1998 - As the sun goes down, the destroyer *USS Nicholson* (DD 982) prepares to launch *Tomahawk* cruise missiles on Iraqi targets. *Nicholson* is currently on a scheduled six-month deployment to the Arabian Gulf in support of *Operation Desert Fox*. U.S. Navy photo by Photographer's Mate 1st Class Todd Cichonowicz. [981218-N-8492C-501]

Oct. 15, 1999 -- The guided missile destroyer *O'Kane* (DDG 77) arrives in its new homeport of Pearl Harbor, Hawaii, after completing a 50-day underway period transiting from Bath, Me. The newest of the Navy's *Arleigh Burke*-class destroyers, *O'Kane* was commissioned in Pearl Harbor on Saturday, 23 Oct. U.S. Navy photo by Photographer's Mate 2nd Class Arlo Abrahamson. [991015-N-5362A-001] Oct. 15, 1999.

THE RITZ-CARLTON HONG KONG

The world's highest hotel, The Ritz-Carlton Hong Kong situated in the upscale West Kowloon enclave, is also the finest 5-star hotel in the Hong Kong area. Located throughout floors 102-118 of the International Commerce Centre (ICC), the seventh tallest building in the world and the highest in Hong Kong, all 312 guest rooms and suites boasts unrivaled views of Victoria Harbor and the glimmering skyline of Hong Kong Island. Inside, soaring architectural elements encrusted with custom glass artwork echo the signature glamour of the city below

www.ingramcontent.com/pod-product-compliance
Lightning Source LLC
LaVergne TN
LVHW051624080426
835511LV00016B/2160